I0006650

Intelligent Influence

AI-Enhanced Marketing Strategies for Global Success

by

Nathan Venture D

Copyright 2023 Well-Being Publishing. All rights reserved.

No part of this book may be reproduced in any form or by any electronic or mechanical means including information storage and retrieval systems, without permission in writing from the author. The only exception is by a reviewer, who may quote short excerpts in a review.

Although the author and publisher have made every effort to ensure that the information in this book was correct at press time, the author and publisher do not assume and hereby disclaim any liability to any party for any loss, damage, or disruption caused by errors or omissions, whether such errors or omissions result from negligence, accident, or any other cause.

This publication is designed to provide accurate and authoritative information with regard to the subject matter covered. It is sold with the understanding that the publisher is not engaged in rendering professional services. If legal advice or other expert assistance is required, the services of a competent professional should be sought.

The fact that an organization or website is referred to in this work as a citation and/or a potential source of further information does not mean that the author or the publisher endorses the information the organization or website may provide or recommendations it may make.

Please remember that Internet websites listed in this work may have changed or disappeared between when this work was written and when it is read.

To You,

Thank you!

Table of Contents

Introduction:
Navigating the AI Revolution in Global Marketing

The integration of artificial intelligence into the vast realms of global marketing is no longer an abstract concept of a distant future; it has become the driving force behind an unprecedented transformation. This evolution has fundamentally altered the landscape of strategies, consumer interactions, and competitive dynamics. As we stand on the brink of a new era, where artificial intelligence intersects with the creativity and intuition of human marketers, we recognize the tremendous potential and the intricate challenges it presents.

Marketing professionals, business leaders, entrepreneurs, and academics are witnessing a period of explosive growth in AI technologies. These tools are unlocking insights into consumer behavior, automating complex processes, and forging personalized connections at scale that were once the stuff of science fiction. These advancements compel us to reassess not only our marketing strategies but also the competencies and ethical frameworks within which we operate.

The dawn of AI in marketing is characterized by machines that learn, predict, and adapt. Consumer behavior is no longer a mystery to be pondered upon; it is analyzed in real-time, fostering business intelligence that is swift and actionable. AI's role in digital marketing has transitioned from a supportive to a pivotal one, shaping decisions that drive growth and ensure relevance in a globalized marketplace teeming with competition and opportunities.

To traverse this AI-driven landscape, intense collaboration between man and machine is necessary for success. The seamless integration of AI into marketing processes demands a shift in mindset, a cultivation of new skill sets, and a firm understanding of the technology's capabilities. Embracing AI is not solely about leveraging technologies but reimagining the role of marketing at the heart of value creation.

Engaging with consumers has always been at the core of marketing. The advance of AI enhances this facet, providing precision through predictive analytics and enabling personalization at an unprecedented scale. Yet with great power comes great responsibility. Ethical considerations, privacy concerns, and the responsible stewardship of consumer data stand as pillars that must uphold customer trust and regulatory compliance.

In the realm of content, AI transforms creation and curation, endowing marketers with the ability to deliver timely, relevant, and context-aware messages. Machine learning does not just streamline processes; it fuels creativity, offering an expanded canvas upon which the art of marketing can be practiced with greater efficiency and impact.

The advertising industry is experiencing a similar metamorphosis. Programmatic advertising, grounded in AI algorithms, is redefining how ads are bought, placed, and targeted. The promise of machine learning here is profound, providing a pathway to measure, analyze, and optimize campaigns with precision and ingenuity.

A social media landscape, teeming with billions of interactions, is brought into focus by AI's ability to sift through chatter, recognize patterns, and engage users. Influencer marketing, too, evolves as AI aids in identifying and partnering with content creators who resonate authentically with target audiences.

Customer experience, often the battleground for differentiation, is enriched as AI comes to life through chatbots, virtual assistants, and bespoke journey mapping. These technologies are not just functionalities; they are becoming ambassadors of the brand, capable of providing real-time personalization that delights and retains customers.

On the cusp of this AI revolution in global marketing, the inquiry into the sanctity of trust and privacy becomes all the more critical. The balance between sophisticated personalization and the privacy of individuals will require marketers to navigate a tightrope where strategic foresight and ethical considerations must intersect with regulatory mandates.

As organizations look to leverage AI to gain competitive advantages globally, the task of localizing strategies while maintaining brand consistency emerges as a complex puzzle. Cultural nuances and localization of AI applications will determine the extent to which global markets can be penetrated and served effectively.

One of the linchpins in this AI-centric marketing future is the people who will drive it. Cultivating a skilled workforce, adept in both the technology and the traditional tenets of marketing, calls for a transformative approach to talent development. Tomorrow's leaders must not only understand AI's potential but also how to harness it ethically and innovatively.

From the vantage point of today's digital marketing ubiquity, we chart the course for the future, looking at AI not just as an aid to marketing but as an intrinsic part of it. The chapters that follow will serve as your compass, guiding you through the digital terrain that AI is shaping, providing insights into its application, and inspiring innovation that will define the next epoch of global marketing.

As we embark on this journey together, let us remain cognizant of the fact that AI in marketing is not just about optimizing campaigns or maximizing efficiencies—it's about creating value in an increasingly interconnected world. It's about understanding the human experience and enhancing it through technology. And with the right knowledge, vision, and approach, marketers can navigate the AI revolution not just successfully, but spectacularly.

The following chapters will illuminate the pathways through which AI is revolutionizing marketing practices, offering a comprehensive look at its impact on consumer behavior, content creation, advertising, social media, customer experiences, and more. The insights provided here are intended to inform, inspire, and elevate your understanding of this transformative technology, ultimately enabling you to lead in an age where AI-driven marketing is not just an advantage but a necessity.

Chapter 1:
The Dawn of AI in Marketing

In the burgeoning narrative of marketing's evolution, artificial intelligence (AI) emerges as a transformative protagonist, heralding an era of unparalleled potential for businesses across the globe. The inception of AI in the marketing realm is not just an incremental step but a quantum leap—a shift that melds the analytical precision of machines with the creative spirit of human strategy. Marketers are now boarding a vessel powered by AI, steering through data oceans with predictive analytics as their compass and personalized content as their sails. As we dissect the anatomy of this digital revolution, the capabilities of AI stand as the backbone, enabling an integration that redefines consumer engagement and paves the way for opportunities that were once inconceivable. It's the dawn of AI in marketing, a thrilling epoch where technology and human insight coalesce to craft experiences that are not only engaging but also echo the unique contours of individual customer journeys. This chapter sets the stage, distilling the essence of AI's inception in marketing and preparing the visionary marketer to harness its expansive potential.

The Evolution of Digital Marketing

Digital marketing's inception hailed a new era for brand and consumer interactions, transforming the exchange from one-way communication to a dynamic, multi-faceted dialogue. As digital platforms burgeoned, so too did the marketing strategies that leveraged them. Email campaigns, banner ads, and rudimentary websites were the first to seed the landscape of digital engagement in the early internet age.

With the emergence of search engines, businesses learned to optimize content for better visibility, and the term 'Search Engine Optimization' (SEO) became a pillar of digital marketing strategies. The focus was not only on being present online but on being discovered. This optimization began quite simply, with keyword stuffing and backlink building, but has since matured into a complex practice that navigates ever-evolving search engine algorithms.

The early 2000s marked the birth of social media platforms and the rapid growth of this new digital territory. Marketers quickly realized the power of connecting with audiences in these spaces and social media marketing was born. Advertisements became conversational, content became sharable, and brand personas adopted a human-like presence within the digital sphere.

As technology advanced, marketers began to leverage data to gain insights into consumer behavior. This marked a shift from mass marketing to a more targeted approach, where ads could be served to specific audiences based on demographics and interests. Consequently, the rise of pay-per-click (PPC) advertising models added a performance-based dimension to the mix, focusing on conversion rates and return on investment (ROI).

Mobile marketing sprang forth as smartphones proliferated. Text messages and mobile apps offered new channels through which marketers could engage consumers with greater immediacy and personalization. Location-based marketing also emerged, unlocking the potential for proximity marketing and real-time offerings.

Content marketing then evolved as marketers discovered the appeal of storytelling and providing value beyond just advertisements. Blogs, infographics, and video content enabled brands to build narratives and share knowledge, fostering a deeper connection with customers and positioning themselves as thought leaders in their respective fields.

With every new opportunity came corresponding analytics, now more detailed and sophisticated than ever. Platforms began to provide real-time insights, allowing marketers to quickly gauge campaign performance and make data-driven adjustments. The push for quantifiable results further tailored the digital marketing landscape, where clicks, impressions, and engagements became key metrics of success.

Enter the era of artificial intelligence (AI); digital marketing began to witness transformative changes. AI-driven algorithms enhanced the ability to predict consumer behavior, and machine learning facilitated the automation of complex tasks, such as personalizing user experiences and optimizing campaign spending.

Programmatic advertising emerged, streamlining the ad buying process and using AI to more effectively target audiences. These systems could analyze vast quantities of data in real time to serve ads to the most relevant user segment, thus maximizing the impact of marketing budgets.

AI also enabled chatbots and virtual assistants, providing a level of customer interaction and service at scale that wasn't previously feasible. These AI-powered tools could handle inquiries, guide customers through a sales funnel, and even provide personalized recommendations without human intervention.

The continuous evolution of AI in digital marketing has brought us to the latest frontier—hyper-personalization. Businesses can now deliver content and offers that are so germane to the individual's preferences and behaviors that the line between physical and digital experiences begins to blur.

With all these advancements, the ethical landscape of marketing has also had to evolve. The use of consumer data, privacy concerns, and the potential for AI to manipulate user behavior have all led to new guidelines, regulations, and discussions around the ethical use of technology in marketing.

As we look to the future, the evolution of digital marketing seems bound to the horizons of AI's capabilities. The interplay between human creativity and machine intelligence will continue to shape how brands communicate, how consumers interact, and how memorable and effective those interactions ultimately are.

The democratization and accessibility of AI tools will foster a new breed of marketers—ones who are not only creative and strategic but also adept in the language of algorithms and data analytics. And as the digital marketing landscape continues to shift, these innovators will be at the forefront, guiding brands through the ever-changing world of consumer engagement.

At the turn of each technological advancement in digital marketing, there is an opportunity—a chance to engage more deeply, measure more acutely, and deliver experiences more personally. As the journey of digital marketing evolution accelerates alongside AI innovations, the potential for brands to forge profound connections with their customers becomes exponentially boundless.

Understanding AI and Its Capabilities

As we delve into the realm of artificial intelligence, it's paramount to comprehend its capabilities and the transformational impact it has on global marketing. AI is like a multifaceted diamond, casting a spectrum of possibilities into the business world.

At its core, AI encompasses systems or machines that mimic human intelligence to perform tasks and can iteratively improve themselves based on the information they collect. For marketers, understanding AI is similar to learning a new language; a language that enables us to converse fluidly with data, glean insights at an unprecedented pace, and execute strategies with precision.

AI holds a mirror to human behavior, reflecting patterns we often overlook. Its ability to process and analyze vast datasets to identify trends and preferences is a game changer for segmentation and targeting. With AI, we can now predict consumer actions before they happen, giving marketers unparalleled foresight.

The integration of machine learning, a subset of AI, allows algorithms to learn from and make decisions based on data. Machine learning can be supervised, unsupervised, or reinforced—each approach with its own strengths in pattern recognition, anomaly detection, and decision-making under uncertainty.

Deep learning, which mimics the neural networks of the human brain, takes these capabilities a notch higher. Marketing applications using deep learning can engage in image and speech recognition, which opens doors to new dimensions of customer interaction and personalization.

Natural language processing (NLP) is another powerful capability of AI, enabling machines to understand, interpret, and generate human language. This means they can manage customer inquiries, automate responses, or analyze social media sentiment, providing insights into customer sentiment.

AI also unlocks the power of predictive analytics in marketing, foreseeing future consumer actions based on historical data. Businesses can adjust their strategies in real-time, aligning with the predicted changes in consumer behavior or market conditions.

Furthermore, AI excels in automation, handling repetitive tasks with speed and accuracy far greater than any human team. This automation extends to email campaigns, content distribution, and even digital ad placements, freeing marketers to focus on strategy and innovation.

AI's role in data visualization is invaluable, transforming complex datasets into understandable, actionable visuals. Marketers can instantly recognize patterns and correlations, which inform more strategic decision-making.

Another significant capability of AI is in recommendation engines. From Netflix to Amazon, these engines enhance the customer experience by personalizing recommendations, keeping users engaged, and increasing the likelihood of conversion.

Chatbots and virtual assistants represent AI's capabilities in customer service. They can provide real-time assistance, understand enquiries, and deliver solutions, elevating the customer support experience to be more efficient and accessible.

In essence, AI's capabilities far exceed merely crunching numbers; it enables a proactive marketing approach, sculpting experiences that are intuitive, and yes, even seemingly human. Artificial intelligence is transforming not just how we market, but also what marketing is fundamentally capable of achieving.

The challenge for marketers then becomes how to harness AI's expansive capabilities responsibly and creatively. To stay competitive in the AI-led marketing frontier, professionals must align AI's potential with their strategic objectives, ensuring that they foster genuine customer engagement and drive business growth through intelligent insights.

Ultimately, understanding AI's capabilities is about recognizing its role as a collaborator in the marketing process. It's about allowing AI to augment—rather than replace—the creativity and emotional intelligence that human marketers bring to the table. This synergy between human intuition and AI's analytical prowess is where the real magic of next-generation marketing lies.

As we progress further into this digital age, AI's influence on marketing will only grow stronger. The capabilities discussed act as the gears of a well-oiled machine, propelling businesses toward more innovative, customer-centric marketing strategies that resonate on a global scale. Our journey through AI in marketing is an opportunity to redefine the relationship between technology, business, and the consumer—in a world where the three are becoming increasingly interconnected.

Integrating AI: A Paradigm Shift

As we venture further into the landscape of AI in marketing, it's essential to grasp that integrating artificial intelligence represents not merely a change in tools or platforms, but a fundamental shift in how we approach marketing. This transformative journey sees us depart from conventional methodologies, steering towards an ecosystem where data is the new linchpin, and agility reigns supreme. Marketers are now architects of a world where predictive analytics and machine learning algorithms inform strategy and creativity.

The embrace of AI in marketing transcends upgrading software or hiring data scientists; it requires a cultural metamorphosis within organizations. Marketing departments are traditionally siloed, with creative and analytical functions often separated. To capitalize on AI's potential, these boundaries need to dissolve, giving rise to interdisciplinary teams versed in both the language of data and the art of persuasion.

A profound paradigm shift involves recognizing the changing role of the consumer in the AI-driven marketplace. Consumers have become active participants, creating data footprints with every digital interaction. AI empowers marketers to interpret these footprints, anticipate needs, and tailor experiences in real-time, crafting a responsive and dynamic brand-consumer relationship.

In essence, integrating AI demands a holistic view. It's about weaving a strategic tapestry where every thread—from email marketing campaigns to customer service queries—is informed by intelligent data analysis. This granular perspective enables marketers to understand consumer nuances in greater depth than ever before, fueling decision-making that's both customer-centric and results-oriented.

What does this transition look like in practice? It begins with education and awareness, ensuring that all stakeholders understand the value proposition of AI. From the C-suite to frontline staff, each member of an organization must recognize how AI can enhance their role and contribute to the overarching goals of the company.

Integration also requires a robust infrastructure. The backbone of AI-driven marketing is a strong technological foundation that is secure, scalable, and sufficiently agile to adapt to evolving AI capabilities. This foundation must be capable of handling vast amounts of data and possess the processing power to analyze it effectively.

Once these foundational elements are in place, the focus shifts to data—its acquisition, management, and utilization. Ethical data collection becomes paramount. Marketers must be vigilant in ensuring that consumer data is gathered transparently, with consent, and used in ways that maintain trust and respect for privacy.

With data at the forefront, AI integration advances to optimization, where algorithms are fine-tuned to detect patterns and predict trends. This predictive capability allows marketers to be proactive rather than reactive, designing campaigns that address consumers' needs before they even articulate them.

However, integrating AI isn't without its challenges. Marketers must confront the dual hurdles of biases in AI systems and the potential for technological obsolescence. Vigilance and continuous learning are critical to ensure that AI-powered marketing strategies remain both fair and cutting-edge.

Importantly, as AI reshapes the marketing industry, it invites a discussion about the ethical implications of its use. Marketers must negotiate the fine balance between personalization and intrusion, ensuring that while they pursue relevance and engagement, they also uphold the dignity and autonomy of the consumer.

Leadership is another critical aspect of AI integration. Leaders in marketing need to champion AI's merits, engage with skeptics, and nurture a culture of innovation. They must also be mindful of potential job displacement fears, guiding teams through upskilling and fostering an environment of continuous professional development.

Collaboration, too, is a cornerstone of AI integration. In an AI-enabled marketing world, cooperation extends beyond internal teams to include external partners, technology providers, and platforms. These relationships ensure that businesses are at the forefront of AI applications and best practices are shared and adapted.

Through it all, central to the success of integrating AI into marketing strategies is a commitment to experimentation and agile methodologies. Marketers must be willing to test, learn, and iterate at a pace that keeps up with the rapid development of AI technologies. This iterative process allows strategies to be refined and ensures that marketing tactics remain relevant and effective.

Finally, at the heart of this shift lies the marketer's role as a storyteller. AI does not diminish the importance of a compelling narrative; it augments it with insights that inform more relatable and impactful stories. In translating data into emotion and connection, AI and human creativity converge, engendering a new era of marketing that is both intelligent and imaginative.

The integration of AI into marketing signifies a tectonic shift in practice and perspective. It's a bold reimagining of the interface between brand and consumer, a synthesis of data science and human insight that heralds a new dawn for the industry. As we progress in this journey, it's incumbent upon us to steer this transformation with thoughtfulness, embracing the promises of AI while thoughtfully addressing the profound changes it brings.

Chapter 2:
AI and Consumer Behavior Analysis

With the sunrise of AI's application in marketing having been heralded, the next frontier emerges as an odyssey through the minds and motivations of consumers, a journey proportional to navigating through a cosmos of data. Artificial Intelligence now stands at the cusp, not merely dabbling in the surface-level tendencies of consumers, but delving deep into the abyss of behavior analysis. Here, AI isn't just a tool; it becomes the cartographer, mapping out the intricate patterns of consumption and illuminating the pathways to decision-making. Through cutting-edge algorithms and machine learning techniques, marketers are empowered to predict consumer needs, tailor individual experiences, and do so at a scale previously unattainable. Marketers may find themselves at the helm of a ship that's equipped to traverse the vast ocean of market dynamics by leveraging predictive analytics, while also anchoring their strategies in the conscientious use of consumer data, ensuring that privacy and ethics guide their sail. In this chapter, we unlock the potential of AI as the quintessential compass in understanding and anticipating the ever-evolving landscape of consumer desires and behaviors, a compass that is recalibrating the very core of targeted marketing.

Predictive Analytics and Consumer Insights

As we journey deeper into the realm of AI and its profound impact on marketing strategies, we come across a potent tool lying at the intersection of technology and psychology: predictive analytics. This data-driven approach, powered by artificial intelligence, holds the key to unlocking vast consumer insights, enabling marketers to not only understand but anticipate consumer behavior.

In essence, predictive analytics refers to the use of data, statistical algorithms, and machine learning techniques to identify the likelihood of future outcomes based on historical data. For marketers, this translates into an unparalleled capacity to forecast consumer decisions and trends. By analyzing patterns and behaviors, businesses can tailor their offerings and interactions to cater to the needs and desires of their customers on an almost individual level.

Within the vast sea of data, predictive analytics zooms in on relevant information that can reveal what, when, and where a consumer is likely to make a purchase. It's not about reading minds; it's about comprehending patterns. The power to foretell can transform campaigns from shots in the dark to targeted strikes that connect with the audience on a personal level, often in real-time.

Take, for instance, the journey of a typical online shopper. Through predictive analytics, we can gauge the likelihood of a cart being abandoned, or a repeat purchase being made, enabling preemptive action to be taken. Whether it's through personalized discounts, reminders, or product recommendations, predictive analytics provides the pathway for more nuanced and effective engagement with consumers.

But it's not just about increasing conversion rates. Predictive analytics is also instrumental in customer retention. By understanding the predictors of churn, companies can devise strategies to keep their customers engaged and satisfied. Tailored experiences, loyalty programs, and proactive customer service can all benefit from insights gleaned through predictive models.

The depth of consumer insights that can be harvested through predictive analytics transcends simple purchase behaviors. It delves deep into unstructured data from social media, customer reviews, and even contact center interactions to sense the underlying sentiments driving consumer preferences and aversions. Sentiment analysis, an AI-powered offshoot of predictive analytics, allows companies to decode the emotional context behind text data, offering a nuanced understanding of public perception pertaining to a brand or product.

Yet, marketers must navigate the ethical boundaries of predictive analytics with care. As consumer insights grow increasingly detailed, so too does the responsibility to handle such data with respect, ensuring privacy and consent are never compromised. Transparency in data usage and adherence to privacy laws are not just legal requirements but foundational pillars of trust between the brand and the consumer.

Another facet to consider is the accuracy and bias inherent in the data. Predictive analytics is only as good as the data fed into it. Flawed or biased data can lead to inaccurate predictions and strategies that may inadvertently alienate or discriminate against certain groups. It's imperative to continuously monitor and refine the data inputs and algorithms to ensure they are equitable and truly reflective of the diverse consumer base.

The integration of predictive analytics also calls for a cultural shift within the marketing team. Data literacy becomes fundamental, with teams needing to understand and interpret complex data sets and models. It requires a blend of technical know-how and marketing acumen to translate data-driven insights into actionable strategies and compelling storytelling that resonates with the target audience.

Moving forward, the AI systems driving predictive analytics will become increasingly sophisticated, learning and evolving with each interaction. This continuous learning loop ensures that consumer insights are not static but dynamic, evolving alongside consumer behavior and market conditions. It is a never-ending quest for deeper understanding and alignment with the customer's wishes and needs.

The democratization of predictive analytics tools means that this technology is no longer the exclusive domain of large corporations with deep pockets. Small and medium-sized enterprises now have the opportunity to harness these capabilities and compete on a more level playing field, making data-informed decisions that were previously inaccessible to them.

Success in utilizing predictive analytics for consumer insights will not come from technology alone. It requires an artful blend of science and creativity – the science of decoding patterns and trends, and the creative application of these insights to craft marketing strategies that are empathetic, engaging, and effective. It's where the science of probability meets the art of marketing, forming a synergy that propels businesses toward growth and competitiveness in the AI-driven marketing landscape.

As we leave the discussion of predictive analytics and consumer insights within AI and marketing strategies, it's clear that the way forward pushes us towards an era where understanding and anticipation walk hand-in-hand. The harnessing of data-driven foresight is not merely an option but a necessity for those who wish to remain at the vanguard of innovation within the complex and ever-changing marketplace.

By embracing the surge of AI-powered predictive analytics, marketers stand on the precipice of unmatched opportunity – to chart courses through the unexplored territories of consumer behavior, to engage with the heartbeat of the market, and to craft campaigns that resonate with precision and foresight. The task ahead is challenging, yet the rewards are boundless for those who dare to navigate the nuanced seas of consumer insights with the compass of predictive analytics guiding the way.

Personalization at Scale

This marks one of the most exciting crossroads where the paths of artificial intelligence and marketing intersect. It's here, within this intricate dance of algorithms and human desires, that businesses are finding unprecedented opportunities to engage with their audiences in ways that were once a marketer's fantasy.

In this multifaceted panorama of digital communications, every individual's preference, behavior, and interaction hold the potential to craft a narrative unique to them, one that speaks to their very core. AI empowers us to analyze incessant streams of data to deliver not just a personalized experience but a distinctively tailored journey to each consumer at scale.

The quintessence of personalization in marketing transcends the mere use of a customer's name. It dives deep into the repository of behavioral data, deciphering needs and predicting wants, all the while crafting a consummate landscape where each message resonates with the recipient. It's a symphony orchestrated by AI, where the right note reaches the right ear at the perfect time.

Every customer touchpoint, be it through email, social media, or a web visit, is a melody of information from which AI can harmonize a personalized experience. Companies are now leveraging machine learning to discern patterns and preferences, subsequently automating communication streams that feel individualized and thoughtfully curated.

Yet, personalization at scale isn't merely an operational boon; it requires astuteness in execution. Marketers must maintain a delicate balance—inundating a customer with overtly personalized content risks tipping the scale towards intrusion. It's the astute marketer who navigates these waters deftly, ensuring relevance without sacrificing the customer's sense of privacy and control.

The advent of AI-driven personalization tools has provided a canvas for A/B testing at unprecedented volumes, thereby fine-tuning messages based on consumer responses. A harmonious loop of feedback and adaptation feeds into the AI, continuously enhancing the accuracy and efficacy of personalized marketing efforts.

Underpinning personalization at scale is the robust infrastructure of data analytics. One must be cognizant of the fact that the treasure trove of data points collected also carries with it the immense responsibility of safeguarding consumer information. Transparency in how data is harnessed, while upholding ethical standards, is non-negotiable and vital to the longevity of personalization efforts.

In the e-commerce domain, personalization at scale has redefined the shopping experience. Product recommendations generated by AI now reflect a deep understanding of the consumer's past interactions, current preferences, and even future needs, potentially predicting desires before the customer even articulates them.

But personalization doesn't stop with product suggestions; it envelops the entire browse-to-purchase journey. Search results, landing pages, and even customer support are intricately woven with personalization threads. This seamless integration elevates the user experience, enhancing loyalty and seeding the grounds for a fruitful, long-term relationship.

This mastery of personalization requires a collaborative effort between various AI technologies. From semantic analysis and natural language processing to machine learning algorithms and neural networks, each plays a pivotal role. Together, they create a cohesive system that discerns complexity and delivers simplicity in the form of personalized consumer engagement.

For personalization at scale to soar, marketers must also appreciate the linguistic and cultural nuances that define each consumer's identity. As companies expand their reach across the globe, AI's capability to tailor experiences despite language barriers and cultural differences becomes invaluable.

Moreover, as the AI grows more sophisticated, the anticipatory power of marketing elevates. Predictive analytics not only guide the creation of personalized content but also determine the optimal timing for engagement. Hence, marketers don't just reach out; they reach out when the consumer is most receptive.

Indeed, personalization at scale envisions a future where marketing is not about broad-spectrum campaigns, but about intimate, meaningful dialogues with each individual. AI serves as the conduit for these dialogues, ensuring that every interaction feels as if it were tailored by human hands.

Personalized marketing at scale, while fueled by technology, must never lose sight of the inherent human element. Behind every data point, every analytical prediction, is a person seeking connection and relevance. As marketers harnessing the power of AI, it is incumbent upon us to honor that humanity in every stratagem we deploy.

As the narrative of personalization at scale unfolds, the potential remains boundless. Marketers stand at the frontier, AI as their compass, guiding them towards a future characterized by connections that empower not just brands, but the very individuals they serve. In this chronicle of marketing evolution, the embrace of AI-driven personalization at scale is not just an advancement—it is the genesis of a marketing renaissance.

Ethical Considerations in Data Usage

As we delve into the complex world of data usage within AI-driven marketing, it's imperative that we examine the underpinnings of ethical practice. Data, the lifeblood of modern marketing strategies, provides invaluable insights but also presents profound ethical dilemmas. As stewards of consumer trust, marketers must navigate the terrain with foresight and responsibility, ensuring that personalization doesn't encroach upon privacy, and that insights are leveraged without exploitation.

Data in marketing is akin to the verdant oilfields of digital engagement—rich, potent, and demanding careful management. Consumers, now more than ever, are sensitive to how their information is aggregated, analyzed, and applied. With great power comes significant responsibility; in the hands of marketers, consumer data can enhance experiences but must always be treated with the utmost respect for personal boundaries and expectations.

The quest for personalized marketing must balance on the fulcrum of ethical consideration. Tailoring marketing messages to individuals can dramatically improve customer satisfaction and drive engagement. However, crossing the line into intrusive or manipulative tactics can swiftly erode the trust that businesses spend years building. This delicate equilibrium requires an ongoing dialogue between evolving technological capabilities and ethical standards.

Consent has emerged as a cornerstone of data ethics. Transparent communication with consumers about what data is collected, how it is used, and whom it's shared with is not only a legal imperative in many jurisdictions but a critical component of trust-building. Explicit opt-in mechanisms and easy-to-understand privacy policies should be non-negotiable elements of any marketing initiative that leverages AI and data analytics.

The diversity of data sources—social media, purchase histories, web interactions—each comes with its own set of ethical concerns. Marketers must be judicious in joining these data streams, ensuring the combined insights don't reveal personal details that consumers have not agreed to share. The aggregation of data amplifies the potential for harm if misused, making rigorous ethical standards all the more essential.

Implicit in the power to predict consumer behavior is the obligation to guard against bias. AI systems are only as unbiased as the data they are fed, and historical data can often reflect systemic inequalities. Marketers need to actively audit and update their algorithms to prevent perpetuating or amplifying biases that could harm user groups or individuals.

Data security is another vital aspect of ethical data usage. As marketers collect and work with increasing volumes of personal data, the potential for breaches grows. Protecting this data from cyber threats is a critical trust factor between consumers and brands. It's not just about having robust security measures in place but also about being ready to respond transparently and swiftly should a breach occur.

The ethical considerations in data usage extend to its lifecycle. How long is consumer data retained, and when is it disposed of? Marketers must craft policies for data retention that respect the consumer's right to be forgotten and mitigate the risks associated with holding data longer than necessary. These policies must be transparent and in alignment with the values of both the consumer and the company.

Accountability sees that marketers don't just comply with the minimum legal standards, but also set higher self-imposed benchmarks for ethical behavior. Adherence to these standards must be measurable and monitored, with clear repercussions for breaches. Accountability mechanisms can often become a source of competitive advantage, as they demonstrate a company's commitment to ethical operations.

One can't discuss data ethics without considering the international playing field. Different countries have varying perspectives and regulations concerning data privacy and ethical use. Global marketers must navigate this complex patchwork of regulations, always aiming for the highest standard rather than the lowest common denominator. This often means developing adaptable frameworks that can be tailored to meet the specific requirements of each jurisdiction.

Equally, the responsibility doesn't rest with marketers alone; organizations must foster an overarching culture of ethics that permeates every department and function. When ethical data usage principles are woven into the organizational fabric, they guide decision-making at every level and safeguard against potential misuse throughout the marketing strategy implementation process.

The exploitation of consumer vulnerabilities is a glaring ethical red flag. Techniques such as dark patterns, where design elements are used to trick users into handing over more information than they intend, must be eschewed in favor of transparent, consumer-friendly approaches. Marketing, at its core, should aim to create value rather than extract it at the expense of the consumer.

In this context, the importance of ongoing education can't be overstressed. As AI technologies evolve, so do the ethical landscapes they inhabit. Marketers must commit to continuous learning, staying abreast of not just the latest tools but also the latest thinking in ethical marketing practice.

Finally, collaboration is essential. Industry-wide standards and best practices can create a more reliable framework for ethical data usage. By working together, marketers can establish norms that not only protect consumers but also enhance the marketing profession's reputation. Collective action has the power to push the industry towards greater transparency, security, and respect for the individual's rights.

In conclusion, the ethics of data usage in marketing are not just a compliance matter but rather a strategic imperative for sustained success. By adhering to ethical practices, we protect not only the consumers but the very industry we serve. As AI continues to reshape the marketing landscape, let's commit to a path of integrity and responsibility, where trust and respect are as critical as the insights gained from the data itself.

Chapter 3:
AI-Driven Content Creation and Curation

As we delve further into the transformative realm of artificial intelligence in marketing, Chapter 3 focuses on the pivotal role AI plays in content creation and curation. The digital landscape is teeming with content, and the ability to stand out hinges on the creation of not only large quantities of material but also on its relevance, quality, and engagement. AI-driven tools are ushering in an era where marketers can leverage natural language processing to generate content that resonates with target audiences, tapping into the subtle nuances of human communication while operating at unparalleled speeds. Similarly, the power of AI to sift through the endless sea of digital information and curate bespoke content streams creates opportunities for brands to provide tailored experiences that capture and retain consumer interest. Together, these technologies are not just facilitators but are catalysts for innovation, challenging marketers to push the boundaries of creativity and strategy in a competition for relevance in an AI-enhanced digital ecosystem.

Natural Language Generation for Marketing

As we take a stride further into the world of AI-driven content creation, we encounter an explosive growth of text-based innovation known as Natural Language Generation (NLG). This technology is transforming the marketing landscape, offering an unprecedented capacity to generate compelling, human-like text at scale. Marketers are beginning to unlock its potential, crafting narratives that not only engage but also resonate deeply with their target audiences.

In the domain of marketing, where content is king, NLG stands as a revolutionary ally. Armed with NLG, marketers can swiftly produce personalized product descriptions, reports, articles, and even narrative analyses that captivate and inform potential customers. This automation in content production is poised to significantly upscale the volume of content without compromising the quality that entices and retains consumers.

The application of NLG in marketing is multifaceted. One such example is email marketing campaigns, where each message can be tailored to the recipient's behavior, preferences, and stage in the customer journey. No longer must marketers adhere to the labor-intensive task of manually segmenting and personalizing communications; NLG systems can dynamically generate content that feels individualized and relevant to each reader.

Moreover, NLG's ability to crunch and interpret complex data and present it in an easily digestible format propels data-driven storytelling to new heights. Marketers harness this capability to present data-rich stories that are both engaging and informative. These narratives allow consumers to understand the context, trends, and insights behind the numbers, fostering trust and credibility in the brand.

The capacity of NLG to continually learn and improve its output based on user interactions is vital for improving customer engagement strategies. Each interaction is an opportunity to refine the nuances of tone, style, and structure to ensure that marketing messages resonate more effectively with diverse audiences over time.

Another transformative aspect of NLG in marketing is A/B testing. Through NLG, marketers can generate a multitude of headlines, product descriptions, or call-to-action prompts, test them in real-time, and pivot quickly to the ones that perform best without human intervention. This form of rapid experimentation leads to data-backed decisions that elevate marketing effectiveness.

Social media, too, reaps the benefits of NLG. Marketers can leverage NLG tools to produce relevant and timely content, ride the wave of trends, and interact with consumers in a manner that feels authentic. These technologies also enable the instantaneous generation of social media posts, responses to trending topics, and engagement with user comments, ensuring that a brand remains top-of-mind and agile in its digital presence.

Content curation is yet another area where NLG provides value. An AI armed with NLG capabilities can craft summaries of existing content or suggest edits and improvements, enhancing the marketer's ability to offer a valuable mix of content to their audience. This not only saves time but also adds depth and richness to the content marketing strategy.

However, while NLG heralds a new era of efficiency and personalization, it's not without its challenges. Striking the balance between automation and authentic human touch is one such challenge. Marketers must ensure that the use of NLG doesn't lead to a homogenized voice that lacks the unique nuances of a brand's identity. It is imperative that NLG be guided and monitored to maintain brand consistency and to inject the human elements of empathy and emotion that resonate with consumers on a deeper level.

To excel in leveraging NLG for marketing, professionals must possess a detailed understanding of its mechanisms, capabilities, and limitations. By forging a symbiotic relationship with NLG tools, marketers can make data-informed decisions swiftly and seamlessly deliver content that engages audiences. This demands that marketers be as skilled in the language of AI as they are in the language of human persuasion.

The ROI of integrating NLG into marketing strategies can be transformative. Marketers who adopt NLG stand to reap increased engagement rates, reduced time-to-market for content, enhanced personalization, and ultimately, boosted conversion rates. The result is a more compelling narrative across all brand touchpoints leading to a stronger, more memorable brand identity.

As we look ahead, the evolution of NLG will likely integrate more sophisticated levels of creativity and emotional intelligence. Marketers who can anticipate these advancements and prepare to use them intricately within their content strategies will gain a competitive edge. Those who overlook NLG's potential may find themselves outpaced in a marketing era that demands agility, personalization, and scalability.

Before diving headlong into NLG, it's essential for marketers to discern the right use cases where this technology can have the most significant impact. It should complement, rather than replace, the creative aspects of marketing that require a human touch. Using NLG in tandem with a marketer's expertise allows for crafting a narrative that marries the best of both worlds.

In conclusion, NLG in marketing is much more than a tool for content generation; it's a transformative force that redefines engagement, narrative control, and the overall consumer journey. Marketers willing to embrace and master NLG stand at the forefront of an AI-powered renaissance in creative storytelling that will set the standard for the industry's future. As we continue to explore the vistas of AI in marketing, NLG emerges not just as an asset but an imperative for those who aspire to lead in the ever-evolving digital landscape.

Curating Content with AI Assistance

In a world inundated with information, curation is as significant as creation. Effective curation involves filtering, categorizing, and presenting content in a meaningful and organized way that adds value for specific audiences. AI assistance streamlines this process, enabling marketers to sift through the noise, identify trends, and offer targeted content. It's not just about automating tasks; it's about enhancing the marketer's capacity to engage and inform.

Imagine the task of curating content for a nuanced, diverse audience. Traditionally, marketers relied heavily on their intuition and experience to assess what content would resonate. Now, AI transforms this landscape through intelligent algorithms that analyze user engagement and identify patterns that might elude even the most seasoned marketers. This is not to say that AI replaces the marketer's role, but rather, it elevates it, allowing professionals to make strategic decisions with data-backed insights at their fingertips.

Interacting symbiotically with AI, marketers can surface content that is not only topical but also contextual. Consider the depth of personalization achievable when content curation is not just about what is trending broadly, but what is relevant to an individual or segment at a particular moment in time. AI's predictive analysis can forecast content relevance based on past user behavior, extracting signals amidst the noise to recommend compelling pieces to individual users or market segments.

Moreover, efficiency in curation is significantly heightened with AI. It can process vast amounts of content at speeds incomprehensible to humans. Where it would take months to assess the impact of content manually, AI platforms can now provide actionable insights in mere moments. With these tools, marketers can rapidly iterate on content strategies and remain dynamic in their approach, adapting quickly to ever-changing market demands and consumer preferences.

Yet, the role of creativity in curation should not be overlooked. While AI excels at sorting and recommending content based on complex algorithms and data sets, the human touch adds nuance and creativity that algorithms cannot replicate. Thus, the intersection of AI and human creativity becomes the sweet spot for curation. Marketers must marry AI's analytical strengths with their own creative instincts and context-awareness—a partnership that promises to transform the potency of curated content.

The ethical considerations of AI-assisted content curation also cannot be understated. With great power comes great responsibility, and AI's capacity to influence through content curation must honor consumer privacy and promote trust. As AI learns from user interactions and behaviors, transparency in how personal data is used and safeguarded is paramount. Marketers must navigate carefully to balance personalization benefits with the demand for privacy, ensuring their AI strategies abide by ethical norms and regulations.

Furthermore, AI curation tools are only as effective as the data they're fed. Inaccuracies or biases in the data can lead to flawed recommendations. Marketers, therefore, have a critical role in overseeing the inputs and training AI systems to be representative and unbiased. This maintains the integrity of the curation process and ensures that the resulting content is diverse and inclusive, reflecting the varied experiences and interests of their audience.

Let's not forget that the ultimate aim of content curation is engagement. AI assists by providing content that it predicts will prompt action—whether that's a like, a share, a comment, or a purchase. As the AI learns which content elicits the desired responses, it refines its curation, creating a feedback loop that continually enhances its precision. Marketers can leverage this loop to produce highly engaging content streams that not only capture but also retain attention.

What does this mean for the future of curation in marketing? It signifies a shift towards more strategic roles where marketers must interpret AI-produced insights and translate them into action. As AI automates the high-volume grunt work of content sifting and sorting, marketers have more freedom to focus on storytelling, brand building, and creative campaigns that resonate on a deeper level with their audiences.

Adopting AI for content curation is not without its challenges. Marketers need to remain vigilant to the context and nuances that AI may not fully comprehend. There's a danger in overly relying on AI, which might lead to homogenized content if not carefully managed. Hence, the skill lies in using AI as a tool rather than a crutch. By understanding its limitations and strengths, marketers can effectively integrate AI to enhance their curation, not dominate it.

Collaboration between different AI systems can also amplify the effectiveness of content curation. Integrating CRM data, social media metrics, and content performance analytics into a cohesive AI model offers a holistic view of what content works where, why, and for whom. It is the insight-driven approach that marks the future of content strategy, rooted in a rich understanding of the consumer, powered by advanced AI analysis.

In summary, curating content with AI assistance is a multi-faceted endeavor that reshapes the marketing landscape. It compels marketers to harness the power of technology to deliver compelling, personalized, and timely content that resonates with their audience. It's an evolution that marries data-driven insights with human creativity, promising a future where marketers are not just communicators but architects of a richer, more dynamic digital experience.

So, as we navigate the AI-infused waters of global marketing, it's essential to approach AI-assisted curation with both a sense of opportunity and caution. It's an art as much as a science, one that necessitates thoughtful integration of technology and the uniquely human capabilities of empathy, context understanding, and ethical judgment. It's within this intersection that content curation with AI assistance will not only thrive but set the stage for marketing innovations yet to come.

The AI-enabled curation landscape is a testament to the transformative potential of technology in marketing. Sustainable and successful implementation, however, will depend on ongoing learning, adaption, and ethical practice. Marketers stand on the brink of a new epoch where AI assistance elevates their role, reshaping the nature of content curation as we know it, ushering in an era of unprecedented connection and understanding in the market space we all inhabit.

Enhancing Creativity with Machine Learning

As we continue to explore the profound impact of AI on the landscape of global marketing, we must turn our attention to the ways in which machine learning is not just a tool for analysis and efficiency, but also an invaluable ally in the realm of creativity. In the dynamic world of marketing, where standing out amid a sea of messages is paramount, creativity remains a cornerstone. Let's delve into how machine learning fosters not just incremental innovation but sometimes leapfrogs what human ingenuity alone could conceive.

Firstly, by harnessing vast amounts of data, machine learning algorithms can identify patterns and trends that might elude even the most astute human marketers. These patterns can form the basis of creative campaigns that are not only unique but also highly relevant to target audiences. Moreover, the iterative nature of machine learning means that each campaign can inform the next, creating a perpetual cycle of creative enhancement and refinement.

Another aspect to consider is the ability of machine learning to generate new ideas. Algorithms designed to create content can produce an array of options more swiftly than a human brainstorming session, from headlines to visual concepts. This abundance of choices can be a catalyst for creative teams, providing a broader starting point for their own ideation. It's important to note, however, that while machine learning can propose myriad ideas, the role of the human marketer is to apply that indefinable creative spark to select and mold these suggestions into compelling narratives that resonate with human emotions and experiences.

Personalization has been a buzzword for some time now, but machine learning takes it to new heights. By tailoring content to increasingly specific segments of an audience, marketers can create experiences that feel personally handcrafted. When customization extends to creating unique visuals or stories for individuals, the connection between brand and consumer becomes deeply creative and personal.

When it comes to content curation, machine learning assists marketers in identifying the content that will engage and hold the attention of their audiences. An algorithm can sift through practically infinite content across the web to discover gems that human curators might miss. This capacity elevates content curation from a logistical task to a creative endeavor, as curators are now empowered to weave together diverse content into a cohesive and engaging narrative.

Product development, too, can see a surge in creativity with the application of machine learning. Consumer feedback, gathered and analyzed at scale, can provide insights leading to innovative product features or entirely new products. Thus, machine learning can inspire creativity that resonates directly with consumer needs and desires.

Moreover, by leveraging predictive models, marketers can anticipate future trends and create groundbreaking campaigns that set the tone for the industry. This preemptive creativity often becomes a benchmark against which other campaigns are measured. Marketers who are the first to leverage these insights can gain a competitive edge by appealing to consumers' desires before they are even fully formed.

In the visual arts, machine learning-enabled tools can create complex patterns and designs that would be time-consuming or impossible for humans to generate manually. These designs can be used in digital media, product packaging, or any visual element of a brand's presence, giving marketers a fresh palette of options for visual engagement.

Collaborative creativity also benefits from machine learning. AI-driven platforms can facilitate idea-sharing and collaboration across geographical and organizational boundaries, breaking down silos and fostering a culture of innovation. When creatives pool their thoughts, feeding into an AI system that learns from each interaction, the result can be truly multifaceted and global creative solutions.

The integration of AI-generated insights into marketing strategies has a transformative effect on the storytelling aspect. Data not only tells marketers what stories might interest their audience but also how these stories can be best structurally composed, which characters resonate most, and what emotions to invoke. Machine learning can dissect what makes a compelling story, allowing marketers to craft narratives with precision and heart.

Moving beyond the ideation phase, machine learning tools are also redefining creative testing. They allow for rapid prototyping and A/B testing of campaigns at a scale previously unattainable. Marketers can now quickly iterate on creative elements, fine-tuning them to perfection, using real-world feedback loops that reduce the risk of costly mistakes and ensure that the final product is as effective as possible.

In the arena of sound, machine learning can analyze music, tone, and voice in marketing materials to advise on the auditory elements that will likely appeal to consumers. Tailoring the soundscape of advertisements can have a subtler but no lesser influence on the effectiveness of creative campaigns.

Similarly, AI's ability to translate and adapt content for different languages and cultures magnifies creative efforts. By understanding linguistic nuances and cultural context, machine learning can craft messaging that retains its core intent while being relevant to diverse audiences. This global perspective enables creativity that not only crosses borders but resonates within them.

Indeed, the integration of machine learning in creative processes signals a shift towards a data-informed yet human-centric approach to marketing. It augments human creativity with computational power, resulting in a blend that transcends what either could achieve alone. It is a decisive step towards crafting marketing strategies that are as emotionally impactful as they are intellectually informed.

However, to capitalise on the creative potential of machine learning, marketers must balance between leaning on data-driven insights and allowing room for human intuition and serendipity. It is this symbiosis that will deliver marketing masterpieces in an AI-driven age. Marketers who understand this balance will not only produce campaigns that are technically impressive but also deeply human.

In conclusion, machine learning in marketing doesn't replace human creativity; instead, it expands it, pushing boundaries and opening new horizons. As machine learning becomes increasingly woven into the fabric of marketing, professionals who embrace it as a partner in the creative process will find themselves at the forefront of inventive, engaging, and profoundly effective campaigns. As we march further into this AI-augmented era, let's remember that at the intersection of data, algorithms, and human creativity lies the potential for marketing magic that truly resonates.

Chapter 4:
Programmatic Advertising and AI

In the dynamic realm of programmatic advertising, AI stands as a transformative force, reshaping how marketers connect with their audiences more accurately and efficiently than ever before. The intersection of algorithmic media buying and machine learning equips professionals with robust tools for navigating the complexity of ad exchanges and real-time bidding. With precision, AI-driven programmatic campaigns dissect voluminous data to deliver targeted advertisements that resonate on a personal level, ensuring that marketing dollars aren't just spent—they're invested. As brands leverage these technologies for unprecedented relevance and reach, they uncover patterns and insights that continuously refine their marketing strategies. Marketers must grasp the nuances of AI's role within programmatic frameworks to maintain a decisive edge in an increasingly competitive and automated marketplace. This chapter will illuminate the formidable synergy of AI and programmatic advertising, delineating a future where the confluence of these marvels not only predicts but also actively shapes consumer behavior and campaign outcomes—redefining marketing efficacy along the way.

The Mechanics of Programmatic Advertising

This dives into the intricate world of digital ad placements, where every click, every impression, and every ad conversion can be meticulously engineered. In the realm of global marketing, programmatic advertising stands as a titan, leveraging the power of AI to position ads with an unprecedented level of precision. It's the vibrant intersection of data science, marketing acumen, and machine learning, all coming together to automate the buying and displaying of ads in real time.

At its core, programmatic advertising involves the automated bidding on advertising inventory in real-time, for the ability to show a specific advertisement to a specific person under specific conditions. Yet, this brief description barely scratches the surface of the depths which this revolutionary technology plumbs. It all starts with the advertisers, who determine their target audience, decide on a budget, and set goals for their ad campaigns. They use what is known as a Demand Side Platform (DSP) to help automate the digital advertising process.

DSPs serve as the nexus where advertisers can buy ad placements digitally across a range of websites, as opposed to the traditional method of negotiating price and placement with individual publishers. They sift through mountains of data and make instantaneous decisions about which ads to buy and how much to pay for them, based on algorithms and real-time bidding (RTB) systems. These algorithms take into account a staggering array of variables, from user demographics to behavioral data, ensuring each ad is tailored to the most relevant audience possible.

The next cog in the programmatic machinery is the Supply Side Platform (SSP), typically utilized by publishers. This platform automates the sale of their ad space to the highest bidder. The SSP is responsible for considering the publishers' minimum prices, filling their available inventory with ads that yield the highest revenue, and ensuring that the content of the ads aligns with the publisher's audience and brand values.

Between the DSP and the SSP lies the Ad Exchange—a digital marketplace where the instantaneous auction of ad space occurs. Each ad impression is auctioned off to the highest bidder in real time, often within the blink of an eye, as a page on a site loads. It's a high-speed trading floor for ad space that operates with incredible efficiency, thanks to the power of AI algorithms.

Data Management Platforms (DMPs) also play a significant role in programmatic advertising by serving as repositories that absorb, categorize, and manage the data used to make programmatic decisions. DMPs collect information from a multitude of sources, including first-party data from within the advertiser's own databases, second-party data shared among partners, or third-party data bought from external providers.

When a user visits a website, cookies and other tracking technologies gather data about them. Advertisers and publishers harness this data to build user profiles that inform their DSP and SSP platforms respectively. The ad exchange puts the ad impression out to tender, and then in milliseconds, the DSP evaluates the impression against the advertiser's targeting criteria and budget, placing a bid accordingly.

For programmatic advertising to work effectively, it requires seamless symbiosis across multiple technological platforms. If a match is found on the ad exchange and the advertiser's bid wins, the ad is then instantly delivered to the prospective customer. The magic of this process is that it is all done in the time it takes for a web page to load, making the placement of ads not just efficient, but virtually invisible to the user's experience.

The effectiveness of programmatic advertising doesn't merely rest on the speed and automation of ad placements, but also on the optimization of campaigns. Machine learning algorithms study the results of ad campaigns in real-time, feeding back into the system which helps in making more informed bids for future ad placements. The system learns which ad placements lead to the highest engagement or conversions, continually refining the strategy to reach marketing goals more effectively.

Transparency and control are also intrinsic to this system. Advertisers can track where their ads are being shown, to whom they are served, and how they perform. They can instantly modify campaigns based on performance data, integrate new data sets for better targeting, and apply optimization instructions to improve the ROI of their campaigns.

While programmatic advertising offers a wealth of opportunities, challenges such as ad fraud, privacy concerns, and the need for high-quality data integrity are also prevalent. Marketers must be vigilant, continually revising and updating their strategies in response to evolving regulations, marketplace conditions, and consumer behaviors.

Despite challenges, the future of programmatic advertising is luminous with potential innovations. AI not only automates processes but also opens the door to creative possibilities in ad personalization, predictive analytics for ad performance, and integrating cross-channel marketing efforts. As machine learning becomes more sophisticated, we will likely see even more nuanced campaign analyses and real-time adjustments that resonate with audiences in ways that seem almost intuitive.

To sum up, the mechanics of programmatic advertising revolve around a virtuosic dance of technology and strategy. It's a dance orchestrated by AI which enables marketers to reach their audiences anywhere in the digital world with unequaled precision and efficiency. In diving into this deep pool, practitioners find that they're not just spectators of the AI revolution in global marketing but active participants in shaping its ongoing evolution. As such, embracing the mechanics of programmatic advertising is not just beneficial, but essential to remain competitive and innovative in an increasingly digitized market landscape.

Through this mastery of programmatic advertising, marketers and business professionals are empowered to leverage AI for substantial and intelligent impact upon their campaigns. The objective is clear: to reach the right person with the right message at the right time, which ultimately drives success in an era of AI-driven global marketing.

In the chapters to come, we will delve into specific facets of programmatic advertising, such as the role of machine learning in ad targeting, the intricacies of campaign measurement and optimization through AI, and the broader influence of programmatic strategies on marketing paradigms. Each component plays a crucial role in catapulting advertisers into new heights of strategic performance, truly embodying the innovative spirit of our times.

Machine Learning in Ad Targeting and Bidding

This stands as a testament to the ingenious application of artificial intelligence in the realm of marketing, where marketers like yourselves strive for precision and efficacy. As we delve into this topic, we tap into the core of programmatic advertising, which has fundamentally altered the landscape of digital ad campaigns, making them more efficient, cost-effective, and intelligent.

Machines learning from data hold the key to anticipating consumer behaviors and automating the decision-making process in advertising. The use of algorithms enables marketers to decipher a complex web of consumer data, extracting actionable insights that fuel the targeting and real-time bidding (RTB) processes inherent to programmatic advertising.

At its essence, machine learning algorithms in ad targeting enable businesses to serve the right ad to the right individual at the ideal moment. This practice, known in the industry as audience targeting, is driven by the analysis of vast datasets that include demographic information, browsing behavior, purchase history, and more. By understanding and anticipating user needs and interests, AI-driven systems can create incredibly precise audience segments.

Beyond segmenting, the granular targeting facilitated by machine learning can significantly elevate the relevance of ads. By predicting which users are more likely to engage with certain content, not only does ad efficiency improve, but the user experience also becomes less intrusive and more meaningful.

The bidding aspect of programmatic advertising, however, takes this game of relevance a step further. Machine learning algorithms are employed to make instantaneous decisions on whether or not to bid for ad space, and at what price, based on the likelihood of the ad's success. RTB, a practice where advertising inventory is bought and sold on a per-impression basis in real-time, hinges on machine learning to operate effectively.

Furthermore, machine learning's predictive power extends to the understanding of the value of an ad impression. It helps in determining not just whether a user might click on an ad, but how this click could potentially translate into a conversion or sale, thus informing the bid amount.

Cost efficiency is another crucial facet machine learning brings to the table. Through sophisticated algorithms, it's possible to optimize campaigns for cost per acquisition (CPA) or return on ad spend (ROAS), ensuring businesses get the maximum value from their advertising dollars.

Dynamic creative optimization (DCO) is also a product of machine learning in programmatic advertising. DCO platforms can alter the creative elements of an ad in real-time to match the preferences and behaviors of the viewer, thereby increasing the ad's engagement rate.

Moving beyond conventional ad targeting, machine learning empowers contextual advertising, which places ads based on the content of a website or a web page. This method circumvents privacy concerns related to user data by focusing on content environments instead of user behaviors.

It's also important to mention how machine learning helps in combating ad fraud—a persistent challenge in digital advertising. AI-driven systems can identify and blacklist fraudulent inventory sources or recognize abnormal patterns that indicate fraudulent activity, therefore protecting campaign integrity and marketers' investments.

As we apply machine learning in ad targeting and bidding, creativity still maintains a vital role. The technology enables the optimization of the media buying process, but a compelling, relevant, and emotionally resonating creative is essential to capture consumer attention and drive performance.

However, with AI at the helm, it's critical to maintain a careful balance of machine-driven decisions and human oversight. Marketers' expertise and intuition remain indispensable, as they guide the overall strategy and ensure that campaigns align with brand values and messaging.

The ethical implications related to data privacy and consumer rights cannot be overlooked. Machine learning in advertising must adhere to evolving regulations and ethical guidelines to maintain consumer trust and comply with the law. Marketers must stay informed about and respect consumers' privacy while leveraging AI to deliver enhanced advertising experiences.

Lastly, embracing machine learning in ad targeting and bidding requires a commitment to continual learning and adaptation. The marketing professionals who actively develop their understanding of AI and engage with these technologies will be best equipped to navigate and lead in this dynamic landscape. The potential of machine learning in marketing is vast; it's a tool that, when wielded with expertise and ethical consideration, can lead to ground-breaking results.

In summary, machine learning is propelling forward the efficiency and intelligence of ad targeting and bidding, bringing about a transformation in the way ads are served and value is maximized. It's a transformative time for marketers, who must stay agile and open to new strategies as they harness the full potential of AI in global marketing endeavors.

Measuring and Optimizing Campaigns with AI

As marketers delve deep into the fabric of programmatic advertising, a critical aspect surfaces that stands to redefine success metrics: Measuring and optimizing campaigns through the invincible power of AI. Programmatic campaigns, with their complex mesh of bid adjustments and audience targeting, demand innovative ways to measure efficacy and return on investment. Artificial intelligence paves a cutting-edge path forward, bringing about a transformation in how we analyze, interpret, and act on marketing data.

In the realm of digital marketing, AI's role in measurement bleeds beyond the traditional analytics. Modern campaigns generate vast swathes of data that can be daunting to navigate. It is here that AI steps in as an indefatigable ally, equipped to parse through data at a scale and speed that is humanly impossible. Marketers can now gain insights in near real-time, allowing decisions to be data-driven and strategically timed.

The optimization of campaigns is no less enhanced by AI. Imagine a scenario where thousands of digital ads are live across various channels, each producing its own set of results. In such a milieu, AI systems can instantaneously adjust bid strategies, pause underperforming ads, and shift resources to top-performing segments. This dynamic optimization ensures that campaigns remain fluid and responsive to consumer behaviors and market changes.

Amidst the avalanche of performance metrics, AI's capability to identify key patterns and trends is revolutionizing campaign reporting. Predictive analytics, one of AI's salient features, empowers marketers to forecast campaign performance based on historical and current data. Such predictions guide informed decisions on budget allocation, potentially boosting campaign ROI dramatically.

AI's attribution modeling furthers the sophistication of measuring campaigns. With an ability to dissect the multitude of touchpoints a customer interacts with before conversion, AI provides a well-rounded view of which channels and tactics are truly effective, enabling reallocation of marketing spends toward the most influential touchpoints.

Performance anomalies don't go unnoticed in the vigilant gaze of AI. Anomalies can indicate both opportunities and threats – a sudden spike in engagement may suggest resonating content, whereas a sharp decline could hint at technical issues or audience fatigue. AI heightens the marketer's ability to act swiftly, either capitalizing on success or mitigating risks.

User engagement metrics, such as time spent on a webpage or interactive elements engaged with, are enhanced through heatmapping and session recordings interpreted by AI. These engagement metrics provide palpable insights into user experience, revealing areas of content that captivate or areas that may require adjustments.

Conversion rate optimization (CRO) can't be talked about without extolling the virtues of AI. From multivariate testing to sophisticated user segmentation, AI brings precision and agility to enhancing the pathways that lead prospects toward conversion. By understanding user behavior deeply and personalizing experiences accordingly, AI maximizes interactions that contribute to the bottom line.

Customer Lifetime Value (CLV) is another dimension where AI shows its strength. By aggregating data across multiple platforms and touchpoints, AI models calculate and predict the long-term value of customers. This insight can shift strategy from short-term conversion goals to fostering long-term relationships and customer retention strategies.

Let us not forget the role of sentiment analysis in optimizing campaigns. AI's ability to discern the tone and sentiment behind customer feedback across the web provides essential insights into brand perception. These sentiments drive campaign messaging and product improvement, ultimately influencing customer satisfaction and loyalty.

AI streamlines A/B testing, one of the tried and true methods of campaign optimization. By automating the test setup and identifying the winning variables more quickly, AI delivers conclusive results with greater speed and accuracy, thereby shortening the feedback loop and expediting marketing improvements.

Visual recognition technology, an AI capability, has found its way into measuring and optimizing campaigns as well. By analyzing images and videos across digital platforms, AI can track brand presence, measure the impact of visual content, and draw correlations with user demographics and behavior.

While AI revolutionizes campaign measurement and optimization, it is essential to keep the human element in the equation. AI acts as a powerful instrument, yet it requires strategic oversight. Marketers must provide context, set goals, and guide AI's learning to ensure alignment with business objectives.

Moreover, the ethical dimension of AI-driven campaigns must be acknowledged. As AI scours data to optimize marketing endeavors, respecting consumer privacy and adhering to regulatory standards is paramount. The success of measurement and optimization depends as much on the technological prowess of AI as on the moral responsibility exercised in its deployment.

In conclusion, the infusion of AI in measuring and optimizing campaigns marks a new era in marketing— one that is precise, responsive, and deeply attuned to the ebb and flow of market dynamics. From predictive analysis to real-time adjustments, AI empowers marketers to reach unprecedented levels of campaign sophistication and effectiveness. As businesses venture further into the AI epoch, the combination of technology and strategic insight sets the stage for marketing marvels that were once mere figments of the imagination.

Chapter 5:
AI in Social Media and Influencer Marketing

Having explored the transformative power of AI in advertising mechanisms, we now delve into the social landscape where AI's synergy with influencer marketing marks an era of unprecedented engagement. Social media, the pulsating heart of modern communication, couples with AI to forge strategies that navigate through the cacophony of content, pinpointing trends, and tailoring conversations that resonate with audiences at a personal level. Influencers, the modern-day heralds, are now selected with an astonishing precision that AI algorithms provide, cutting through the clutter of vanity metrics to reveal true conveyors of brand messages. These technological advancements allow for an evolution in sentiment analysis and brand monitoring, offering real-time feedback that is deftly granular, ensuring that brands stay attuned to the public perception in ways that were once unattainable. In this chapter, we'll explore how AI not only revolutionizes our approach but is also becoming an indispensable ally in crafting genuine, dynamic, and ultimately successful social media and influencer campaigns that speak directly to the heart of what it means to engage in the digital agora.

Harnessing AI for Social Media Strategies

Understanding how to leverage artificial intelligence in social media marketing is no longer an adjunct skill—it's a necessity. AI tools have become an intrinsic part of how we understand, interact with, and influence social media users. As algorithms evolve, so too must our strategies, adapting in a way that not only seeks to engage with our audiences but also to anticipate their needs and behaviors.

Social media, the ever-pulsing lifeline of global conversation, presents a robust landscape for marketing professionals. The introduction of AI into this realm amplifies opportunities for brands to connect with individuals on a more personal level. AI's role in social media strategy is multifaceted, offering an ability to analyze large datasets, identify trends, and calibrate content delivery with unprecedented precision.

At the heart of social media lies content – the golden currency. AI boasts the capability to generate and curate content at a scale unthinkable to the human marketer. From crafting engaging posts tailored to the nuances of each platform to suggesting optimal posting times, AI is redefining how we populate our feeds. It can analyze performance metrics from past posts to inform future content, ensuring that each image, video, or text snippet resonates soundly with its intended audience.

Beyond content creation, AI can personalize user experiences on social platforms, distinguishing among individuals' interests and engagement patterns. Predictive analytics, powered by machine learning algorithms, can forecast what users are likely to consume, share, and respond to. This anticipatory approach allows your brand to be several steps ahead, crafting experiences that feel intuitively aligned with user expectations.

User engagement is another critical aspect AI dramatically enhances. By analyzing interactions, AI can help marketers understand not just the 'what' but the 'why' behind user behaviors. These insights pave the way for developing more impactful engagement strategies that drive meaningful conversations and, ultimately, conversions.

AI can also streamline and improve customer service on social platforms. Through the use of intelligent chatbots and virtual assistants, businesses can provide real-time assistance. These AI-driven interfaces are continually learning and adapting to provide more accurate and helpful responses, reflecting an understanding and personalization that resemble human interaction.

One of the most potent tools in the social media marketer's arsenal is targeted advertising. AI elevates this practice by processing massive amounts of data to identify the best audience segments for specific messages. It helps in optimizing ad spend by ensuring that the people most likely to be interested in your product or service see your ads.

Social media is a breeding ground for trends. AI tools are adept at spotting emerging trends before they become mainstream. By tapping into this ability, brands can position themselves as thought leaders and innovators, staying ahead of the curve and engaging audiences through topical content.

With the growth of influencer marketing, AI becomes indispensable in identifying and partnering with influencers whose values and audiences align with your brand. Not only can AI help pinpoint these influencers, but it also can monitor the efficacy of these partnerships, offering real-time insights into campaign performance.

Sentiment analysis, an AI function, interprets the mood and opinions expressed about a brand on social media. By utilizing sentiment analysis, a company can gauge public perception, manage its reputation more effectively, and respond swiftly to any negative sentiment before it escalates.

Competition is fierce on social platforms, and standing out requires innovation. AI promotes such innovation by providing the tools for experimentation without the traditional risks. Marketers can test different content types, messaging, and strategies quickly, drawing conclusions from actual data rather than speculation.

Another aspect where AI proves essential is in measuring the impact of social media strategies. With sophisticated analysis capabilities, AI helps to determine the return on investment for particular tactics, giving a clear picture of what works and what does not, thus enabling a dynamic approach to strategy development.

Lastly, while implementing AI in your social media strategies can provide tremendous benefits, it is imperative to maintain ethical considerations. Transparency about data usage, protecting user privacy, and avoiding manipulative tactics are all considerations that must be woven into your AI strategy to maintain consumer trust.

In conclusion, the potential for AI to revolutionize social media strategies is boundless. It's not only transforming how we execute marketing tactics but also enhancing our understanding of the consumer landscape and our own creative processes. As we look to the future, embracing AI in social media is not just an option; it's the essential path forward for those who aim to lead in the competitive world of digital marketing.

As we venture deeper into the world of AI-enhanced social media, it becomes unmistakably clear that the convergence of technology and creativity is the linchpin of success. Marketers who can skillfully balance the analytical power of AI with the human touch that resonates on a personal level will champion the social media arenas of tomorrow.

AI Tools for Influencer Identification and Engagement

Influencer marketing, once a novel concept, has grown into a mainstay of modern brand strategy. As marketers, our challenge lies in pinpointing the perfect catalysts for our campaigns—individuals who resonate with our audience and embody our brand's values. AI tools have emerged as invaluable allies in this pursuit, bringing efficiency and precision to the art of influencer identification and engagement.

The convergence of AI with influencer marketing begins with the identification process. A suite of sophisticated AI-powered platforms now offers the capability to sift through social media's vast expanses, using advanced algorithms to categorize and rank potential influencers. These tools assess not only follower count but also a myriad of nuanced variables such as engagement rates, audience demographics, and content style, ensuring a comprehensive analysis.

Engagement is the cornerstone of effective influencer partnerships, and AI is revolutionizing this facet as well. Today's platforms extend far beyond mere discovery, facilitating the entire lifecycle of influencer relationships. From first contact to campaign tracking, AI systems automate communication, streamline workflow, and track the metrics that matter most, saving precious time while maximizing ROI.

AI's might is in its data-driven approach, transforming influencer selection from a guessing game into a science. It processes historical data to predict future performance, tapping into past collaborations, audience reactions, and market trends to guide decision-making. With this predictive prowess, brands can be more strategic in their collaborations, aligning with influencers who are likely to deliver optimal results.

Another key dimension is the alignment of values and image. AI tools delve into the sentiments expressed in an influencer's content and the reactions of their audience, ensuring brands connect with partners who truly share their ethos. This in-depth approach helps construct campaigns that are authentic and thus more likely to succeed in today's discerning market.

When it comes to engagement, AI platforms are not mere matchmakers. They orchestrate the confluence of content with audience tendencies, suggesting optimal posting times, content formats, and even engagement strategies tailored to individual influencers and their followers. This personalized guidance can significantly amplify the impact of influencer collaborations.

In building these partnerships, negotiation is key, and AI can provide a wealth of relevant data points to inform these discussions. By analyzing market rates and influencer performance metrics, AI gives brands the upper hand in negotiations, equipping them with the insight needed to secure fair pricing and clear expectations.

The integration of AI doesn't stop at the campaign launch. Real-time performance tracking is essential, and AI analytics platforms offer a live view of campaign metrics, from engagement rates to detailed audience reach. This not only ensures campaigns are on track but also allows for agile adjustments in response to ongoing data.

Furthermore, AI enhances our ability to scale influencer marketing efforts. Manual processes can hamper growth, but with AI, the possibilities for expansion are vastly extended. This scalability is a boon for businesses aiming to widen their influencer net without proportionally increasing their workforce.

Embedded within these tools is advanced Machine Learning technology that continuously improves its recommendations and strategies based on outcomes. This self-optimizing feature means that the more a brand engages in influencer marketing, the smarter the AI system becomes, further refining future campaigns.

Brand safety is another area of concern expertly navigated with the aid of AI. Monitoring the online presence and content of influencers can be arduous, but AI tools vigilantly scan for potential red flags or content that may not align with a brand's image and standards, proactively preventing reputational risk.

While AI's capabilities are vast, the human touch remains vital for authentic connections. AI serves to complement and enrich human decision-making, not to replace it. Its role in identifying and engaging influencers is to streamline and fortify the process, not to dehumanize it. It's the harmonious blend of technology and human intuition that yields the most fruitful influencer partnerships.

In leveraging AI for influencer marketing, we also unlock predictive insights about audience behavior and preferences. These insights guide not just whom we partner with but also help forecast the trends and shifts within our consumer base. It's a powerful loop where influencer engagement informs consumer understanding and vice versa.

Finally, it's worth noting that the technology landscape is ever-evolving, and what's cutting-edge today may be commonplace tomorrow. Keeping abreast of the latest developments in AI for influencer marketing is not just advisable, it's imperative for those looking to sustain a competitive edge. The willingness to adapt and integrate fresh AI innovations will distinguish the leaders in influencer marketing from the laggards.

In conclusion, AI tools for influencer identification and engagement represent a transformative shift in how we approach this critical element of marketing. In transforming vast datasets into actionable intelligence, these tools empower marketers to forge more productive, impactful influencer connections. As we navigate the dynamic terrain of global marketing, AI stands as a monumental ally, driving us toward smarter strategies and more profound engagements, ultimately propelling brand narratives forward in an increasingly connected world.

Sentiment Analysis and Brand Monitoring

As we delve deeper into the integration of AI within the sphere of social media and influencer marketing, the importance of maintaining a vigilant eye on brand perception becomes paramount. Sentiment analysis emerges as a key player in brand monitoring, leveraging the power of machine learning to decode the nuances of human emotion behind social media interactions, customer reviews, and other digital footprints left by consumers.

Brand monitoring, traditionally a labor-intensive process of manually tracking brand mentions across various platforms, is continually revolutionized by AI. Marketers no longer sift through enormous datasets aimlessly but are now equipped with tools that intelligently identify and analyze conversations, sentiments, and trends related to their brand in real-time. The key lies in comprehending not just the prevalence of mentions but the context and emotional tone they carry.

Sentiment analysis, at its core, is the automated process of interpreting and categorizing opinions expressed in text data. This advanced form of textual analysis allows for a nuanced understanding of customer sentiments, ranging from positive, negative, to neutral, and even detecting subtler emotional cues such as sarcasm or enthusiasm. As brands thrive on customer perception, the insights obtained from sentiment analysis can drive critical business decisions, tailoring marketing strategies more effectively to meet consumer needs.

AI-driven sentiment analysis tools process colossal volumes of data with a precision unmatchable by human efforts. They employ natural language processing (NLP) techniques to dissect the structure and meaning of language used across digital platforms, whether it's a tweet, a blog post, or a product review. AI algorithms continually learn and adapt to the intricacies of language, becoming more accurate over time and thus providing increasingly valuable insights.

In the context of brand monitoring, sentiment analysis can be leveraged to gauge the impact of marketing campaigns, product launches, or any notable company actions. The feedback loop is accelerated exponentially—a brand can now identify consumer reactions almost instantaneously, allowing them to respond to crises, adapt strategies, or capitalize on positive sentiment in a swift and calculated manner.

Monitoring sentiment also enables brands to track their health over time. By systematically analyzing shifts in sentiment, companies can detect emerging issues before they snowball into full-blown controversies, or they can identify opportunities for building stronger customer relationships and loyalty.

Another realm where sentiment analysis contributes is competitive analysis. By examining not only their own brand sentiment but also that of their competitors, businesses can benchmark performance, uncover competitive advantages, or learn from the challenges faced by others within their industry. This data-driven approach infuses objectivity into what has traditionally been a subjective domain of business intelligence.

Deep dives into sentiment analysis reveal correlations between sentiment trends and business outcomes such as sales figures or stock performances. These correlations enable predictive models which can forecast potential market movements based on the changing tides of public opinion. Forward-thinking brands use this analysis to tweak marketing efforts, manage inventory, and prepare customer service to handle impending demand variations.

Amidst this ocean of data, AI assists in identifying influential voices and key opinion leaders—essential for influencer marketing strategies. Sentiment analysis can unveil which influencers genuinely resonate with audiences and endorse products with perceivable sincerity. This optimization ensures that marketing dollars are spent where the highest engagement and positive sentiment are assured.

Ethical considerations also come into play with sentiment analysis. Navigating the fine line between insightful analysis and invasive surveillance is critical to maintain customer trust. Brands must be transparent about data collection and harnessing AI while respecting privacy and adhering to data protection regulations. It's a delicate balance, utilizing powerful tools for insight without trespassing on individual rights.

Harnessing sentiment analysis for brand monitoring inevitably leads to a richer customer profile. By understanding emotional reactions, marketers can design more empathetic and personalized experiences. But beyond the operational aspects, there's an opportunity for brand alignment with customer values—establishing a deeper, almost symbiotic relationship that transcends the transactional nature of business.

As the data pool grows and AI tools evolve, sentiment analysis will undoubtedly become more sophisticated. Emergent technologies such as emotion AI seek to go beyond text, analyzing voice inflections and facial expressions to gain a fuller picture of sentiment. This expansion paints a future where AI interprets human emotion in a multimodal fashion, across various channels for a composite view of brand sentiment.

To summarize, sentiment analysis and brand monitoring represent a formidable fusion of AI capability and marketing acumen, with the potential to transform brand management. The rich insights harvested lead to proactive strategies, operations attuned to consumer needs, and a dynamic brand image that can navigate the ebullient waters of public opinion with grace.

The future promises even greater advancements in AI that will further refine sentiment analysis, making the integration of these tools not just beneficial but indispensable for brands seeking to maintain relevance and resonance in a rapidly evolving digital landscape. AI-powered sentiment analysis offers marketers not just a lens, but a telescope to the hearts and minds of consumers.

Thus, as we continue to harness the power of AI, it's crucial for brands to remain agile, receptive, and above all, empathetic to the voices of their consumers. Sentiment analysis and brand monitoring are more than technological achievements; they are the beacons guiding brands towards a future where understanding and engaging with customers on a deeper level isn't just possible—it's the new standard.

Chapter 6:
AI-Powered Customer Experience and Support

In the realm of modern marketing's transformation, Chapter 6 delves into the profound impact of artificial intelligence on customer experience and support. As today's consumers expect instant, personalized service, AI stands at the forefront, revolutionizing how brands cater to their customers. Utilizing sophisticated chatbots and virtual assistants, companies can provide round-the-clock support, ensuring inquiries and concerns are addressed with near-human levels of understanding but without the constraints of human availability. Far beyond the scope of scripted responses, these AI systems are adept at learning from interactions to enhance future communications. Concurrently, AI's role in customer journey mapping provides marketers with rich, nuanced insights, enabling the crafting of a tailored and engaging experience for each customer. This precision in targeting means that real-time personalization and recommendations align seamlessly with an individual's preferences and behaviors, fostering a sense of relevance and deepening brand loyalty. Chapter 6 not only showcases how AI is elevating customer interactions to unprecedented levels of customization and convenience but also exemplifies the necessity for businesses to adapt to this technological wave to maintain a competitive edge in a market driven by exceptional customer experiences.

Chatbots and Virtual Assistants

These are integral to how brands are flipping the script in customer interaction and service. It is within the golden threads of AI-powered chatbots and virtual assistants that businesses are weaving a new fabric of customer engagement. These AI entities represent more than just automated responses; they embody the seamless blend of efficiency and personalization that is reshaping the customer journey in real time.

Imagine an 'always-on' world where customer queries are met with immediate, insightful, and accurate responses. That's the pivotal role chatbots and virtual assistants are playing in today's marketing landscape. They aren't the robotic voice prompts of yesteryear that tested one's patience. Today's AI-driven assistants are conversational and adaptive, leveraging the power of natural language processing (NLP) to understand and interpret human speech with remarkable accuracy.

In the domain of customer service, chatbots are swiftly transitioning from being mere novelty to necessity. They offer an unparalleled level of availability, providing round-the-clock support that matches today's consumer expectations for instantaneity. Their ability to manage a high volume of inquiries simultaneously reduces wait times and liberates human agents to tackle more complex and sensitive issues — all contributing to an uplift in customer satisfaction and loyalty.

Moreover, virtual assistants are becoming sophisticated enough to engage in proactive customer service. By analyzing consumer behavior and purchase history, they can anticipate needs and offer relevant recommendations. This not only leads to increased revenue but also to a deeper, more personal connection with the customer, further ingrained by AI's relentless learning curve, where each interaction hones its ability to serve even better than before.

Marketing professionals are recognizing the bountiful opportunities AI-driven chatbots provide. These virtual entities become ambassadors of the brand's voice, tone, and values, offering a consistent messaging across various platforms and touchpoints. Brands can design and refine their chatbot interactions to deliver experiences that are uniquely their own, echoing corporate identity while ensuring relevance to the user's needs and queries.

Furthermore, virtual assistants are a treasured source of consumer data, offering insights into common questions, concerns, and preferences. This data can be fed back into the marketing strategy, fine-tuning campaigns and identifying potential areas for product or service enhancement. AI's machine learning component ensures that this data isn't just raw numbers but transformed into actionable intelligence, empowering marketers to make informed, strategic decisions.

In this intertwining of AI with customer experience, personalization has taken center stage. Chatbots are equipped to deliver personalized interactions at scale, potentially remembering past conversations and preferences to tailor future communications. This feels like a conversation with a knowledgeable friend rather than a transactional exchange, fostering a sense of loyalty and trust between customer and brand.

Operating in the global market calls for a nuanced understanding of cultural norms and linguistics — an area where AI virtual assistants are making strides. Multilingual capabilities are increasingly prevalent, allowing brands to transcend borders and offer competent support without the heavy overhead of a multilingual human staff. Moreover, the cultural adaptability of AI means marketing messages delivered through these bots can be nuanced and tailored to respect cultural sensitivities and traditions.

However, it's not just customer-facing roles where virtual assistants shine. Internally, they are revolutionizing how marketing teams operate, automating repetitive tasks such as scheduling, analytics reporting, and data management. This automation liberates the creative minds within marketing to focus on what they do best — innovating and pushing the boundaries of brand storytelling.

The conversation around chatbots and virtual assistants isn't without its challenges. Consumer trust in AI varies, and there remains a critical need for transparent data practices and ethically designed conversational algorithms that respect user privacy. Regulatory landscapes are evolving too, and compliance is paramount to ensure that these AI tools are used responsibly.

Looking ahead, continuing advancements in AI mean that the capabilities of chatbots and virtual assistants are only set to broaden. We're moving towards a future where these AI entities can conduct more complex conversations, execute transactions, and provide even finer personalized experiences. Their evolution will be paramount in driving customer engagement and satisfaction, thus directly impacting brands' bottom lines.

In conclusion, emboldening the customer experience with AI through chatbots and virtual assistants is a vivid illustration of innovation in global marketing. As these technologies mature, they will form the backbone of customer service and engagement strategies, offering seamless, personalized, and culturally nuanced interactions that connect brands with their customers more deeply than ever before. The dawn of AI in marketing has indeed yielded a powerful tool, and those who harness it will navigate the future of global marketing with a distinctive edge.

AI in Customer Journey Mapping

This delineates a process critical to fostering deep connections with consumers — mapping the customer journey. Mastery in this area is not just advantageous; it's essential in the current marketing landscape, where the customer's path to purchase is increasingly complex and nonlinear.

Imagine a world where you know precisely what your customer is thinking, the exact moment they're inclined to make a purchase or what might cause them to hesitate. Artificial Intelligence (AI), when deployed in customer journey mapping, brings this scenario closer to reality than ever before. By analyzing huge amounts of data and recognizing patterns that are indiscernible to the human eye, AI presents marketers with unprecedented insight into every stage of the consumer journey.

The beauty of customer journey mapping with AI lies in its ability to digest and interpret vast datasets that encompass various touchpoints, interactions, and customer behaviors. Unlike traditional journey maps, AI-powered maps are dynamic. They constantly evolve as new data inputs are received, ensuring that the journey map is always reflective of the current state of the consumer experience.

Take, for example, predictive analytics, a cornerstone of AI's value in customer journey mapping. It enables businesses to forecast future customer behaviors based on historical data. Predictive models delve into past purchase behavior, online browsing patterns, and social media engagement to predict the likelihood of a customer's future actions. This predictive power allows marketers to craft strategies that meet customers at the most opportune moments.

The ability to personalize experiences is perhaps the most powerful aspect of AI in journey mapping. AI algorithms are capable of sifting through data to tailor marketing messages and offers to individual consumers. Rather than sending out broad, generic campaigns, marketers can use AI to identify the unique needs and preferences of each customer and craft customized messages that are much more likely to resonate.

AI tools can also enrich customer journey mapping by identifying micro-moments, those instances when consumers turn to their devices for quick answers to their immediate needs. Whether they're looking up reviews, comparing prices, or searching for nearby stores, AI helps marketers to understand and capitalize on these critical decision points.

Engagement tracking is another realm where AI proves invaluable. With it, marketers can quantify and analyze each interaction a customer has with their brand across different channels. This comprehensive analysis allows businesses to not only see the journey but also understand the effectiveness of their marketing efforts at each touchpoint. It's the difference between having a roadmap and a GPS system with live traffic updates — the latter being far more useful in navigating a journey efficiently.

Then, there's the issue of scaling these insights. Manually creating customer journey maps for each customer segment would be a laborious task. AI can automate this process, quickly generating nuanced maps for different segments or even individual customers at a scale that's manageable for marketers.

However, implementing AI in customer journey mapping is not free of challenges. One of the key hurdles is the integration of different data sources. Since the data feeding into the AI comes from multiple touchpoints—social media, email, website, physical stores, customer service interactions—it's crucial to have an integrated system that consolidates all this data.

Another critical challenge is ensuring data quality. AI models are only as good as the data they're trained on. Inaccurate or biased data can lead to misguided insights, so there's a profound need for systems that can cleanse and validate data before it's used for mapping.

The ethics of data usage also come into play. With such granular insight into customer behavior, the balance between personalized marketing and privacy invasion becomes delicate. Marketers must navigate this ethically, ensuring transparency and consent from customers while leveraging AI to its fullest potential.

Moreover, as AI journey maps become more sophisticated, they can also integrate sentiment analysis. By interpreting customer emotions through their feedback, social media comments, and other engagements, marketers can understand the emotional triggers at various journey stages. This allows for a more nuanced approach to enhancing the customer experience.

Real-time personalization is another front opened by AI in customer journey mapping. Instead of reacting to customer needs, AI can proactively adjust the journey in real-time, presenting opportunities for upselling, cross-selling, or offering support before a customer even asks for it.

In conclusion, AI in customer journey mapping is transformative. It conveys not just the path a customer takes but also the context around their decisions, the emotional undertones of their interactions and predicts future behavior. However, the very power of AI to draw such detailed maps also mandates a responsibility to use this insight judiciously, ethically, and in a way that amplifies customer trust.

In a world that's more connected than ever, the companies that can harness AI effectively to map the customer journey are the ones that will navigate the waters of modern marketing with precision, continually adapting to the ever-changing needs and behaviors of their audience. They'll set the course for success in a future where AI isn't just a tool but a central component of customer-centric marketing strategy.

Real-Time Personalization and Recommendations

In an ever-accelerating world, where the attention span of consumers is shrinking, the importance of real-time personalization and recommendations in marketing cannot be overstated. Marketers, business professionals, and entrepreneurs alike are turning to AI to craft experiences that are not merely tailored, but acutely synchronized with each consumer's immediate context and needs. This agility in marketing strategy serves as a significant competitive advantage, ensuring engagement and conversion at unprecedented rates.

Imagine a world where each customer interaction is an opportunity for a brand to learn, adapt, and respond instantly. AI makes this possible by analyzing consumer behavior, preferences, and even current environmental factors to provide personalized experiences on-the-fly. With AI, dynamic content personalization becomes the norm, with marketing messages finely tuned to the individual's exact point in the customer journey. It's not about creating a single path to purchase but rather a multitude of evolving paths that adapt in real time.

The heart of this real-time revolution lies in the sophisticated algorithms backed by machine learning. These algorithms process vast amounts of data quickly, discerning patterns and preferences with a degree of precision that human analysis could never achieve independently. With this capacity, AI systems can predict what a customer is likely to want next, even before the customer has fully formed the desire themselves. The result is a level of service and satisfaction that can dramatically boost brand loyalty and lifetime value.

Engagement metrics soar as recommendations become increasingly relevant. The AI systems are not only recommending products or services that the user is likely to enjoy but are doing so at the optimal moment for influencing purchasing decisions. Real-time personalization also allows for the seamless integration of cross-selling and up-selling opportunities, presenting items or services complementary to the customer's current selection or search history.

However, personalization extends beyond product suggestions. It encompasses the complete user experience. This includes customized landing pages, individualized email marketing, bespoke social media interactions, and even personalized discounts and promotions. Each touchpoint is an avenue for a highly personalized engagement, fostering a deep connection between the consumer and the brand.

Furthermore, in physical retail spaces, AI-enabled devices and applications are enhancing the in-store experience. By using real-time data and AI analysis, retailers can deliver personalized recommendations through mobile apps or in-store displays the moment a customer enters a specific zone or interacts with a product. This harmonious blend of digital intelligence with physical retailing is crafting a new paradigm for customer engagement.

The immediacy of AI-driven personalization also delivers exceptional value in customer support. AI chatbots and virtual assistants are equipped to anticipate customer concerns and offer real-time solutions, advice, or product recommendations that feel both considerate and intuitive. This doesn't just satisfy customers; it delights them, creating a narrative where the brand's responsiveness is key to the story of their day.

On the flip side, leveraging AI for real-time personalization and recommendations presents marketers with a formidable challenge: maintaining a balance between being helpful and becoming intrusive. As AI refines its understanding of consumer data, the line between personalized service and privacy concerns grows thinner. It's crucial for marketers to navigate this aspect with care, ensuring consent and protecting customer data to maintain trust and compliance with regulatory standards.

Granularity is another aspect to consider. With AI's ability to segment audiences down to individuals, marketers can craft micro-segmentation strategies, targeting niche customer profiles with highly specialized offerings. This approach dramatically enhances the relevance and appeal of marketing messages, translating into higher conversion rates and a more effective utilization of marketing budgets.

Integration with other marketing systems is also vital. AI-driven personalization systems need to work hand-in-hand with customer relationship management (CRM) platforms, content management systems (CMS), and other marketing technologies to ensure a consistent and coherent customer journey across all touchpoints. Seamless integration ensures that AI's recommendations resonate with established customer narratives, thus heightening the impact of real-time personalization.

Testing and optimization must be continuous. AI systems are adept at learning and improving over time, but they require ongoing monitoring to ensure they remain aligned with brand values and customer satisfaction goals. A/B testing and other experimental frameworks can guide marketers in refining their AI personalization strategies for even greater efficacy.

Furthermore, the ethical use of AI in marketing, especially pertaining to real-time personalization and recommendations, necessitates transparency. Customers should be made aware that AI is being used to enhance their experience and must have the option to control what data is utilized and to what extent they wish to receive personalized content. Ethical transparency is not merely a legal obligation but a cornerstone of customer trust.

Looking beyond simple transactions, real-time personalization wrought by AI can lead to a shift in corporate culture. As businesses begin to recognize the value of treating each customer as an individual, with unique desires and expectations, organizational approaches to product development, customer service, and marketing strategy are transformed. This kind of empathetic, responsive approach to business can forge deep emotional connections with customers, superseding the transactional nature of traditional commerce.

In conclusion, AI demonstrates transformative power in the realm of real-time personalization and recommendations. It sets the stage for a marketing landscape characterized by immediate, intuitive, and profoundly individualized interactions between brands and consumers. As AI's role in global marketing strategies continues to expand, mastering the art of AI-driven personalization will become not just a competitive edge, but a basic expectation of consumers in the digital age.

Chapter 7:
The Future of SEO: AI and Search Algorithms

As we pivot from immersive customer experiences to the pivotal cogs of search engine optimization (SEO), it's essential to grasp the seismic shift towards an AI-centric future. In this chapter, our compass is set to demystify the sophisticated dances between artificial intelligence and the ever-evolving search algorithms that define online visibility. It's here that marketers must sharpen their foresight, as voice search optimization begins to echo through the corridors of strategy, compelling us to reimagine keywords and context in a world where queries become conversations. The intricacies of AI will not merely tweak but revolutionize current search mechanisms, rendering yesterday's SEO playbooks quaint relics. Content crafters will unlock new realms of possibilities, learning to weave narratives that resonate not only with human emotions but also with the meticulous scrutiny of AI search evaluators. Forging ahead, our mandate is clear: to synthesize human creativity with machine precision in constructing content landscapes that AI deems worthy of ranking supremacy. This chapter heralds the onset of an era where understanding and staying ahead of algorithmic patterns is not just strategy—it's survival.

Voice Search Optimization

As the world steadily adapts to the conveniences of voice-assisted technologies, it becomes paramount for businesses to align their search engine optimization strategies with voice search capabilities. Voice search optimization is no longer a footnote in digital marketing strategies but a cornerstone in designing a future-proof plan. In this section, we delve into the nuances that make voice search a unique terrain to conquer in the realm of Artificial Intelligence and global marketing.

Voice search is a technology that enables users to use their voice to command digital devices and query search engines. This rising trend has led us into an era where keyword stuffing and traditional SEO tactics take the back seat to conversational queries and natural language processing. The proliferation of smartphones, smart speakers like Amazon's Echo and Google Home, and an array of other voice-enabled devices has catapulted voice search optimization to the forefront of strategic marketing imperatives.

For marketers, the marriage between AI and voice search offers a wealth of insights and challenges. To fully embrace this change, we must begin by understanding user behavior. Voice search queries tend to be longer, more colloquial, and phrased as questions. This marks a shift from typed queries, which are often briefer and more fragmented. Marketers need to adjust their keyword strategies by incorporating long-tail keywords and creating content that answers direct questions posed by potential customers.

Local searches become increasingly important within voice search optimization. Consumers using voice search are often seeking location-based information—a trend that necessitates local SEO optimizations. This includes claiming and optimizing your Google My Business listing, ensuring your location information is up to date across all platforms, and embedding local keywords within your content.

Site speed too cannot be ignored. Voice search-powered devices present users with prompt answers, signifying that sites with better load times are favored in voice search rankings. The importance of optimizing technical SEO cannot be overstated—an AI-driven marketing strategy must ensure websites are primed for the quickest deliveries.

Developing content that aligns with the conversational nature of voice search is crucial. Creating FAQ pages, blog posts that directly address user questions, and ensuring content is structured in a manner that mimics human dialogue can improve a site's visibility in voice search results.

With the rise of voice search, the importance of structured data and rich snippets becomes emphatic. Apply schema markup to help search engines understand and display specific information about your business. This enables AI-driven systems to easily parse your content and surface it for relevant voice queries.

Moving beyond the technical aspects, voice search optimization also prompts a need for a more human-centric approach. The tonality and style of the content must feel natural and coherent. Your brand voice should smoothly interact with AI technologies, maintaining consistency and personality that resonates with your audience even in the absence of a visual interface.

Accessibility plays a pivotal role in voice search. Ensuring your content can be easily interpreted by AI and is optimized for voice search is key in becoming inclusive. This speaks not only to a broader audience reach but also reflects a commitment to diversity and inclusivity—traits that modern consumers value greatly.

Security must be a top priority when optimizing for voice search. With increased data vulnerabilities associated with voice commands, a parallel focus on safeguarding user data is essential. Strategies around voice search must integrate robust security measures to protect against potential breaches that may erode consumer trust.

Continual optimization is the cornerstone of voice search readiness. As AI technologies evolve, so too must optimization strategies. Marketers need to be agile, constantly testing and adapting to the shifting behaviors of consumers and advancements in AI-driven search algorithms.

Analyzing and understanding voice search data will direct smarter marketing decisions. By leveraging AI to dissect complex voice search data, marketers can gain a competitive edge through nuanced customer insights that inform content creation, user experience improvements, and personalized marketing strategies.

Voice search optimization transcends the boundaries of search engines and website content—it seeps into every customer touchpoint. Therefore, it must be integrated into a holistic AI-driven marketing strategy that considers email marketing scripts, social media interactions, and even customer service responses.

To remain competitive in a global market where voice search popularity continues to grow, businesses must not only anticipate the needs of their audience but arrive there before the competition does. From understanding the dynamics of different languages and dialects worldwide to ensuring your optimization strategies are culturally sensitive, voice search optimization is a microcosm of the larger global marketing picture.

Embracing AI in voice search is not about overhauling your strategy overnight—it's about creating space for your marketing strategies to evolve with technology. Look toward the future with a mindset of learning and adaptability. As tools and platforms emerge, so too will opportunities for businesses to engage with their customers through more natural and intuitive means. This is where voice search optimization becomes not just an option, but an imperative.

In sum, voice search optimization is a multifaceted challenge requiring a sophisticated, nuanced approach. Marketers must blend the insights offered by AI with the finesse of human touch to create an optimized, voice-search-friendly presence that not only resonates with customers but also drives business results. In the AI age, this blend of technology and humanity will define the next horizon of global marketing success.

AI and the Evolution of Search Engine Algorithms

Search engines have become the lighthouses of the digital age—guiding users through the vast ocean of information to the content most relevant to their queries. But like all technology, search engines do not remain static; they evolve, and at the forefront of this evolution is artificial intelligence (AI). AI has drastically altered the landscape of search algorithms, creating a profound impact on global marketing strategies.

As we peel back the layers of search engine optimization (SEO), we uncover a dynamic world where AI has redefined the fundamentals of algorithmic ranking systems. These intelligent algorithms now understand context, anticipate user intent, and learn from interactions to deliver more accurate search results. This paradigm shift has elevated the importance of creating content that is not only keyword-rich but also contextually relevant and valuable to users.

Historically, search engine algorithms were heavily reliant on technical signals like keyword density and backlinks. However, the introduction of AI-powered algorithms like Google's RankBrain signals a shift towards semantic search. It's no longer just about the frequency of a term on a page, but about the overall topic and its relevant subtopics, as well as the quality of the information provided.

AI's involvement means that search engines are getting better at understanding natural language. This advancement gives rise to a more conversational approach in content creation known as voice search optimization. The ability to recognize and process natural language queries is a monumental leap from the simplistic keyword matching of the past.

Another area where AI shapes the search engine landscape is personalization. Now, search results are increasingly customized to individual users based on their search history, location, and even device usage. For businesses, this underscores the importance of personalized marketing strategies that can adapt to the preferences of various users.

Latent Semantic Indexing (LSI) and related technologies have been incorporated into search algorithms, too. They assist in understanding the relationship between different terms and concepts within content. This has a significant implication for content creators, who must ensure a rich, interconnected web of topics to leverage the full potential of AI-influenced search algorithms.

The evolution of search engine algorithms has also heightened the significance of user engagement metrics. User behavior signals, such as click-through rates, time spent on a page, and bounce rates, feed back into the AI system, helping it determine the value that users derive from a piece of content.

As marketers, understanding these ever-changing algorithms can feel like chasing a moving target. Yet, embracing AI in SEO strategy becomes not just advantageous but essential. Marketers must equip themselves with the latest tools and techniques to analyze and adapt to algorithmic changes. These include AI-based SEO platforms that track algorithm updates and recommend adjustments for optimal content visibility.

In terms of global competitiveness, the universal language of SEO is now spoken with an AI accent. Multi-language content optimization is necessary, considering that AI-driven algorithms transcend language barriers, enabling broader content reach and more inclusive engagement across global populations.

Machine learning, a subset of AI, continuously refines search algorithms. In this learning process, the algorithm iterates over vast data sets, making incremental improvements to result rankings. This non-stop optimization process means that the criteria for high-ranking content can evolve daily. Marketers are no longer just content creators; they are now students of an ever-learning AI system.

The proliferation of AI in search engines also has exciting implications for predictive search. By analyzing past search behavior and other user data, AI can forecast user needs and provide content that meets those needs before the user even conducts a search. This proactive approach to content deployment could revolutionize how brands engage with consumers.

However, marketers must also navigate the ethical considerations that come with AI-influenced search algorithms. An over-reliance on data-driven strategies may lead to biases or exclusion of certain demographics if not properly managed. This consideration calls for a balance between leveraging AI's capabilities and maintaining the human touch in marketing.

Ultimately, the integration of AI into search algorithms heralds a new age of digital marketing. Marketers must embrace a culture of continuous learning and agility to remain relevant. The content must be crafted with a deep understanding of both technology and the human elements—creativity, empathy, and values—that connect brands to their audiences.

By staying abreast of AI developments in the search engine space, marketers can make strategic decisions that anticipate changes rather than react to them. This approach empowers businesses to be thought leaders, setting the standard for content that is not just found but resonates and inspires.

As we delve deeper into this AI-induced renaissance of search engines, we find that the essence of marketing remains the same: to reach the right audience with the right message at the right time. AI does not change this goal; it simply propels us into a future where achieving it is more intricate but also filled with greater possibilities. Embracing this evolution is not only beneficial for a brand's online presence but also pivotal in carving a niche in the ever-expanding digital marketplace.

Creating AI-Friendly Content

The emergence of AI in global marketing has not only augmented the efficiency of operations but has also redefined the content creation process. To harness the power of AI and ensure the visibility of your content in an increasingly automated digital landscape, it's essential to understand and master the art of crafting AI-friendly content. This isn't about writing for machines; it's about striking a harmonious balance where content appeals to both artificial intelligence algorithms and human readers.

But what does AI-friendly content look like? For starters, it involves a deep understanding of the intricacies behind search algorithms, which have now evolved to prioritize context, relevance, and user engagement over simple keyword stuffing. AI-powered search engines are designed to recognize value for the user and rank content accordingly. This recognition hinges, in part, on the strategic use of keywords, sure, but also on the creation of comprehensive content that addresses the searchers' intent in a conversational and informative manner.

Furthermore, the structure of your content plays a crucial role. AI systems prefer well-organized and logically outlined articles, which makes it important to use headings and subheadings effectively. This not only enhances readability for your human audience but also allows AI crawlers to better understand and index your content. When these systems can clearly discern the hierarchy and flow of your content, the chances of higher ranking in search results significantly improve.

In tune with the structural aspect, readability must be given due consideration. A compromise must be struck between sophistication and simplicity — your content should be easily digestible, yet rich with information. Short sentences and paragraphs can help the content seem less daunting, while the use of transitional phrases can seamlessly guide the reader — and AI — through the narrative you're weaving.

While written content is a major focus, one can't ignore the rise of visual content and its significance in the AI realm. High-quality images, videos, and infographics not only make content more engaging for human viewers but when tagged with relevant and descriptive meta-data, they become a feast for AI-algorithms. Alt-text for images and proper file naming conventions are just the tip of the iceberg when it comes to preparing visual content for an AI-enhanced future.

Another cornerstone of AI-friendly content is the interlinking of relevant articles and pages within your website. This doesn't only improve user experience by providing them with additional valuable information but also allows AI algorithms to establish connections across your site, appraising its breadth and depth of knowledge in your field.

Consistent updates and refinements to content are also essential; static pages may be forgotten by algorithms in favor of fresher, regularly updated content. This strategy tells AI that your website is not only active but also working to provide current and valuable insights, thus maintaining its relevancy.

User engagement metrics are often interpreted by AI as signals of content quality. Encouraging user comments, shares, and time spent on the page can indirectly influence how algorithms perceive and rank your content. Crafting content that spurs interaction and discussion goes a long way not only in community building but also in reinforcing AI alignment.

As mobile usage continues to dominate internet browsing, creating mobile-optimized content becomes indispensably linked to being AI-friendly. Fast-loading pages, responsive designs, and touch-friendly navigation all factor into how AI views your content's accessibility and, by extension, its relevance and quality.

Localized content for global markets isn't just about translation, but about cultural context, local idioms, and nuances that resonate with the target audience. AI's role in global marketing stretches to linguistic nuances and geographic pertinence, which enhances the user experience and by default, aligns well with AI's inherent goal of providing tailored content.

With the rise of voice search, crafting content that reflects natural speech patterns is increasingly paramount. As AI technologies like virtual assistants become more prominent, they also become a larger source of web queries. Your content needs to answer questions people might ask in a normal conversation, not just the written word.

The incorporation of structured data through schema markup extends the comprehensibility of your content to AI. By annotating your content with this standardized format, you're making it possible for AI to more easily parse and understand the relationships between different elements and concepts within your content. This can significantly enhance visibility in search engine results pages through rich snippets and knowledge graphs.

An often-overlooked aspect is the integration of AI tools in the creation process itself. AI-driven keyword tools, content optimization software, and trend analysis platforms can not only help align your content with current SEO standards but also anticipate changes in the information-scape. Utilizing these tools allows marketers to maintain a pulse on what is both currently effective and what is looming on the horizon, ensuring the content stays ahead of the curve.

In the broader sense, creating AI-friendly content is akin to future-proofing your marketing efforts. It's about laying a strong foundation in an environment where algorithms are becoming increasingly smart and intuitive. By feeding these systems the right information in the right format, your content is less likely to be misinterpreted or overlooked by the AI that now governs much of our digital experience.

In summary, the convergence of AI with content creation is not looming, it's already here. Embracing AI-friendly content practices require a blend of technological savvy, marketing acumen, and an empathetic understanding of the human element behind every search query. Content that is designed to meet the needs of both AI algorithms and human intellect stands the best chance of performing well in a marketing ecosystem that continues to evolve at an unprecedented pace. The goal is simple yet complex: to create content that is as much a resource to the algorithm as it is to the human heart and mind.

Chapter 8:
E-commerce and AI: Transforming
Online Shopping

The digital marketplace, once a static arena of simple transactions, is undergoing a seismic transformation, as artificial intelligence redefines the essence of online shopping. E-commerce businesses are now harnessing AI to revolutionize inventory and supply chain management, ensuring unparalleled efficiency and customer satisfaction. The nuance of AI's capabilities extends into crafting highly customized shopping experiences that resonate deeply with individual consumer desires and preferences. By analyzing vast datasets, AI predicts and responds to buyer behavior with unmatched precision—turning browsing into buying. Visual and voice search commerce, spearheaded by sophisticated AI algorithms, is setting a new standard for convenience; they are transforming the way we interact with online stores, breaking down barriers for those who can't navigate traditional interfaces. Through the strategic infusion of AI technology, e-commerce platforms not only boast strengthened operational fluidity, but they also promise a future where each shopping experience feels as personal and distinct as the consumer behind the screen.

AI in Inventory and Supply Chain Management

Influential transformations within the domain of global marketing are increasingly defined by the finely woven threads of artificial intelligence, especially in how companies manage their inventory and orchestrate supply chain logistics. As we delve into this landscape, we observe that AI systems are now indispensable tools for brands seeking to maintain a competitive edge through optimization and prescience in stock control and resource allocation.

The integration of AI in inventory management allows businesses to transcend the traditional approaches that relied heavily on human estimation and error-prone forecasting. With sophisticated algorithms capable of parsing through historical data, analyzing seasonal trends, and predicting future demands with remarkable accuracy, supply chains become markedly more efficient. AI does not merely suggest the quantity of products to stock but also advises on optimal reorder points and intervals, thereby minimizing stockouts and excess inventory simultaneously.

Supply chain management harnesses AI to create an interconnected ecosystem where each node, from the manufacturer to the distribution center to the retail shelf, communicates in real-time. This symphony of data-driven insights facilitates proactive decisions, ensuring that supply meets demand across all touchpoints. Additionally, such systems can detect anomalies that might indicate delays or disruptions, enabling businesses to enact contingency plans with agility.

Furthermore, AI applications in logistics can optimize routes for transportation, improve load planning, and predict and manage shipping delays. This sort of dynamic routing not only conserves resources by reducing fuel consumption and travel time but also betters compliance with increasingly stringent environmental regulations.

The role of machine learning in refining these predictions and optimizing stock levels through continuous learning ought to be underscored. As these systems ingest more data, their forecasts become more precise, leading to a virtuous cycle of improvement that perpetuates enhanced supply chain resilience.

There is also a significant impact on cost reduction when deploying AI in supply chains. By identifying patterns and operational bottlenecks, AI enables businesses to address inefficiencies, leading to cost savings that can be transformative for a company's bottom line. Through demand forecasting and price optimization, AI tools can make informed recommendations on purchasing raw materials and managing inventory holding costs.

Inventory visibility is another aspect where AI brings immense value. With real-time tracking and predictive analytics, companies attain a granular view of inventory levels across multiple warehouses and retail locations. This visibility is paramount to orchestrating an omnichannel strategy where inventory movement is fluid and responsive to consumer behavior.

Supplier relationship management (SRM) is enhanced through AI by enabling companies to evaluate supplier performance comprehensively. Predictive analytics can alert procurement managers to potential issues with suppliers before they affect the supply chain, allowing for a proactive rather than reactive approach to supplier management.

AI's role extends to inventory audits and compliance, where it can automate and streamline processes that are otherwise time-consuming and prone to error. With the use of sensors, image recognition, and robotic process automation, stock levels can be continuously monitored without human intervention, significantly lowering the risk of loss and theft.

In the sphere of product lifecycle management, AI can predict the optimal time to introduce new products or phase out older ones by analyzing market trends and consumer preferences. By aligning inventory decisions with strategic product launches and retirements, brands can enhance product success rates and avoid costly overproduction.

The influence of AI also permeates the realms of procurement. Through deep learning and cognitive analytics, AI platforms can analyze vast amounts of supplier data and market conditions to make procurement recommendations, such as when to buy materials to take advantage of favorable pricing or to mitigate risk.

Nevertheless, one must consider the implications of predictive accuracy. AI thrives on data, and the success of these systems hinges on the quality and quantity of the input data. Thus, companies must establish stringent data governance practices to ensure that the algorithms producing stock and supply chain management insights operate on clean, relevant, and comprehensive datasets.

Collaboration and communication among stakeholders in the supply chain are fostered by AI-driven platforms. These systems allow multiple players within the supply chain to align goals and share insights that contribute to a cohesive strategy, essential for responding effectively to market changes and consumer needs.

Crucially, for marketers, AI in inventory and supply chain management doesn't merely concern logistics and storage; it's integral to ensuring that the customer promise is fulfilled. Whether it's ensuring that the right products are in place for a campaign, or managing deliveries to meet customer expectations, the seamless and cost-effective flow managed by AI is a cornerstone of the modern customer experience.

To encapsulate, the potent capabilities of AI in inventory and supply chain management are revolutionizing global marketing strategies. They confer upon businesses the ability to operate with unparalleled efficiency, agility, and intelligence, resulting in elevated levels of customer satisfaction and robust economic health. It's through these strategic incorporations that businesses can leverage AI not merely as a tool but as a transformative force shaping the future of global trade and commerce.

Customized Shopping Experiences

In an age when consumers are flooded with choices, delivering a tailored shopping experience isn't just appreciated; it's expected. Brands that understand and harness the power of AI to offer bespoke services are seeing their efforts translate into increased customer loyalty and sales.

Customization is the cornerstone of modern e-commerce. Shifting from a one-size-fits-all approach, AI is empowering brands to create individualized experiences that cater to the unique preferences of each shopper. By collating and analyzing vast datasets, businesses are not just predicting consumer behavior but also shaping it.

Imagine entering a virtual store where the layout, product recommendations, and even the promotions are aligned with your tastes and buying history. This isn't the shopping of tomorrow; it's happening now. Through machine learning algorithms, AI tracks and learns from each customer's interactions, continuously refining the shopping experience to make it more personal and engaging.

It's more than just recommending products. AI enables dynamic pricing, where the cost of an item might adjust depending on demand, availability, and the customer's propensity to purchase. Brands are increasingly using this strategy to optimize sales and inventory, ensuring a win-win situation for both the business and the consumer.

Personalized marketing messages are another way AI customizes the shopping experience. Businesses send tailored emails, push notifications, and even social media messages based on individual customer data. These targeted campaigns result in higher conversion rates as they resonate more effectively with the recipient's interests and needs.

Virtual fitting rooms exemplify AI's transformative potential in e-commerce. Using augmented reality, customers can try on clothes, accessories, or even makeup virtually, reducing the guesswork associated with online shopping and significantly lowering return rates.

Customer service has also felt the touch of customization. AI-powered chatbots provide 24/7 support, offering responses tailored to individual queries and customer profiles. These bots can handle a multitude of tasks from fielding basic questions to guiding customers through complex purchase processes.

Customized search functions further streamline the shopping journey. AI algorithms are capable of learning user preferences to prioritize search results according to the shopper's past behavior, making product discovery quicker and more relevant.

The role of AI isn't limited to the frontend; it also optimizes backend operations for a smoother customer experience. AI systems can predict stock requirements, automate reordering processes, and manage logistics, ensuring products are available when and where they're needed.

Despite the benefits, customization by AI doesn't come without its challenges. Privacy remains a paramount concern. Brands must navigate the fine line between personalization and invasion of privacy.

Transparent data practices and respecting customer preferences are critical to maintaining trust.

As technology progresses, the scope for customization also expands. AI is beginning to predict not just what customers want now but also what they might need in the future. Predictive analytics is revolutionizing inventory management by suggesting new product lines and different models based on emerging trends.

Additionally, the evolution of customized shopping experiences isn't uniform across the globe. Cultural nuances and regional preferences play a significant role in shaping how personalization is applied. Marketers must be attuned to these differences to ensure successful implementation.

For brands, the opportunity within customized shopping experiences is vast. Long-term brand loyalty and increased spending can often be attributed to customers feeling understood and valued. When customers perceive that their tastes and preferences are being catered to, their relationship with the brand deepens.

In conclusion, the integration of AI into customized shopping experiences signals a shift in how businesses interact with their consumers. As we navigate through the continuously evolving digital marketplace, those who embrace AI's capabilities in offering tailored experiences stand to gain a competitive edge.

For marketers, this means sharpening their understanding of AI technology and its applications in e-commerce. By doing so, they arm themselves with the tools necessary to design not just a product or a campaign, but a shopping journey that resonates on a personal level with each customer. In an era where competition is only a click away, providing a customized shopping experience could be the defining factor that sets a brand apart.

Visual and Voice Commerce

As we delve into the transformative powers of artificial intelligence within the realm of e-commerce, a fascinating frontier emerges at the crossroads of innovative engagements: visual and voice commerce. These interfaces represent the convergence of user-centric design and AI sophistication, heralding a new era where convenience and seamlessness take center stage.

A key element of this innovative commerce stream is the growth of voice-activated assistants, which have rooted themselves into the fabric of daily life. Their capability to interpret and action on human commands has revolutionized the way we think of shopping. No longer do consumers need to wade through pages of products; a simple vocal instruction can initiate a complex search for items, compare prices, and even finalize purchases, thanks to the integration of AI.

In the vein of visual commerce, image recognition technology has made remarkable strides. It allows users to take photos of products they encounter in the real world and, through AI algorithms, find similar or identical products in an online inventory. This tangibility—a bridge between the physical and digital realms—entices customer engagement and shapes a new pattern of impulse buying, rooted in immediacy and visual appeal.

Visual and voice commerce are not just novel entry points into consumer transactions; they are channels loaded with data, ripe for analysis. The nuances of consumer speech patterns, accents, and visual preferences unearth layers of consumer insights. Savvy marketers harness this information to create deeper personalization strategies, further endearing their brands to the consumer's lifestyle and habits.

At the backend, these technologies leverage Natural Language Processing (NLP) and Machine Learning (ML) to better understand and predict customer behavior. NLP interprets and responds to voice commands whereas ML continually refines the process, learning from each interaction to enhance recommendation systems and search functionalities.

The rapid adoption of smart speakers and mobile devices equipped with voice assistants like Siri, Alexa, and Google Assistant has made voice commerce a conduit that businesses can't afford to ignore. For users, the attraction lies in the hands-free, frictionless experience—a considerable advantage for multitaskers and visually impaired customers, further emphasizing inclusive marketing practices.

Yet amidst the momentum, there exist challenges pivotal to the success of visual and voice commerce. One such challenge is establishing trust as customers lean on technology to make recommendations previously sought from human support. AI must navigate the subtleties of consumer skepticism and the innate need for assurance, aspiring to match, if not surpass, the human touch.

Another hurdle pertains to search engine optimization (SEO) for voice queries. SEO tactics must now account for conversational language used in voice searches, which tend to be longer and more specific than text-based queries. As the landscape shifts, marketers must recalibrate their strategies to capture the distinct intent behind spoken requests.

Fusing visual with voice commerce is the next evolutionary leap; envision a scenario where a customer describes a desired product verbally and is instantly presented with a visual assortment of options curated by AI. This powerful combination can enhance user experiences, offering a holistic and intuitive shopping journey, pivotal to customer satisfaction.

The value of analytics in visual and voice commerce cannot be overstated. Marketers gain access to rich layers of voice intonation and visual preference data, providing insights beyond traditional text analytics. The strategic advantage lies in deciphering these cues to align product development and marketing tactics with unvoiced consumer expectations.

Visually, the use of augmented reality (AR) in commerce further bridges the gap between virtual and reality. Consumers can 'place' products in their own space before purchase, reducing the guesswork and increasing confidence in buying decisions—something that voice commerce alone cannot offer.

Collaboration and partnerships are essential for the proliferation of visual and voice commerce ecosystems. Large tech companies provide the platforms, but it is up to creative businesses to design experiences that leverage these platforms in engaging, customer-centric ways. Financial investments in this technology are simultaneously rising, indicating burgeoning confidence in its market potential.

Moreover, global scalability of visual and voice commerce depends on the AI's ability to adapt to multilingual challenges. The integration must be seamless across various languages and dialects if a truly global customer base is to be catered to. This underlines the drive for AI that is not just intelligent but culturally aware and sensitive.

Security concerns also take center stage as voice commerce, in particular, raises questions about verification processes. Consumers might worry about the misuse or accidental use of their voice commands leading to unintended purchases, highlighting the necessity for robust authentication mechanisms to be baked into the core of voice commerce platforms.

In the grand tapestry of e-commerce, visual and voice commerce represent innovative threads weaving through the consumer experience, promising to blend utility with the magic of AI. For businesses vying for competitive advantage, mastering these domains offers a transformative opportunity, but it demands astute attention to the evolving narrative of consumer behavior, security, and personalization.

As we continue to explore the contours of AI in e-commerce, recognizing the profound interplay between visual and voice commerce becomes imperative for any entity looking to not just survive but thrive in the ceaselessly dynamic market spaces of tomorrow. Harnessing the power of AI in these realms could very well redefine the essence of shopping as we know it, blending intuitive interfaces with intelligent analytics to cater to the consumer of the future.

Chapter 9:
AI, Privacy, and Trust in Marketing

As we advance into the era where artificial intelligence (AI) touches all facets of marketing, understanding and navigating the intricate landscape of privacy and trust becomes paramount for marketers. Personalization, powered by AI, has been a game-changer in delivering relevant and engaging customer experiences. However, it's this same granularity of customer knowledge that raises red flags for privacy advocates and consumers alike. The delicate dance between leveraging AI for personalized marketing, while safeguarding consumer privacy, calls for a nuanced approach—one where transparency isn't just a buzzword, but a foundational element of customer interactions. Establishing trust in this AI-driven context goes beyond assuring customers about data security; it's about consistently demonstrating ethical behavior in data collection and use. As regulatory bodies tighten compliance requirements, a marketer's ability to marry AI capabilities with a steadfast commitment to privacy will not only be a legal mandate but a competitive differentiator. Mastering this balance means embracing a forward-thinking mindset that always places consumer respect at the heart of AI strategies, ensuring that customer-centricity isn't lost amidst the algorithms.

Balancing Personalization with Privacy

In the landscape of AI-fueled marketing, a keen equilibrium must be struck between providing tailored experiences and remaining vigilant guardians of consumer privacy. Marketers are walking a tightrope, needing to deliver sufficient relevance to engage consumers, while simultaneously honoring their desire for personal data security. As we delve into this topic, exploring the facets of this balancing act becomes essential to heed the responsibility that comes with the power of AI-driven personalization.

The enchantment of personalization lies in its potency to resonate deeply with consumers, crafting messages and experiences that align with individual preferences and behaviors. AI, with its unparalleled analytical capabilities, offers marketers the tools to parse vast data sets, unveiling actionable insights that underpin personalization. It's these insights that fuel the delivery of content, products, and services tailored like never before.

However, the same data that empowers personalization also raises the specter of surveillance—if not handled with care. Consumers are increasingly aware of their digital footprints and the potential misuse of their information. Many have grown weary of invasive advertising and are skeptical of the intentions behind data collection. Hence, it's not just a matter of legal compliance but of ethical practice to ensure privacy is not an afterthought.

Significantly, trust becomes the cornerstone of this precarious balance. Earning customer trust hinges on transparency about the data being collected, how it's being used, and what control the consumer has over this process. Informing customers about the benefits they receive in exchange for their data can alleviate concerns, but this message must be delivered with clarity and sincerity.

Forward-looking companies are investing in privacy by design approaches, embedding privacy into their systems from ground up rather than as an add-on feature. This proactive stance not only mitigates risks but also positions these companies as trailblazers in the best practices of data ethics.

Furthermore, demonstrating adherence to international data protection regulations like GDPR and CCPA is a tangible way to show commitment to privacy. It's no longer just about compliance; it's about shaping a corporate culture that values privacy as a fundamental component of its business model.

Yet, for all these measures, the question persists: how can personalization be delivered without contravening privacy? AI technologies must be trained to anonymize and aggregate data, ensuring individual identifiers are not exposed. Machine learning algorithms can be engineered to discard unnecessary information automatically, focusing only on data that enhances customer experience without compromising individual privacy.

The importance of customer feedback loops cannot be overstated. Engagement with customers to gather their input on personalization preferences fosters a sense of control and partnership. It empowers consumers to set their boundaries, which in turn, bolsters their comfort and trust in how their data is leveraged.

In the AI ecosystem, the ethical use of data is also a competitive differentiator. Brands that are transparent, responsible, and customer-centric in their data practices can elevate their market position and engender loyalty.

Reference architectures and responsible AI frameworks are emerging as blueprints for companies to follow. These frameworks guide the responsible deployment of AI systems, ensuring ethical, transparent, and accountable uses of data at every stage of consumer interaction.

Consumers are more likely to share their data when they perceive a clear benefit. It's essential for marketers to communicate that value proposition effectively. When personalization enhances the customer experience—such as through more accurate recommendations or time-saving offers—it's seen in a positive light, and the value exchange becomes mutually beneficial.

Collaborative filtering is an example of a technique that leverages crowd-sourced data to generate recommendations while maintaining user anonymity. Such methods can strike a balance between personalization and privacy, showing that AI doesn't have to cross-and shouldn't-customer boundaries to be effective.

Audit trails and automated compliance checks are also part of the privacy equation. Implementing systems that record how data is being handled not only supports regulatory compliance, but also provides reassurance to stakeholders that privacy is being taken seriously.

Empowered consumers demand control over their privacy settings. Companies that offer customizable privacy features, allowing users to fine-tune how much of their data is used and for what purposes, will stand out for their respectful approach to personalization.

Ultimately, marketers must embrace the dual role they play as both champions of brand growth and protectors of customer privacy. Companies that successfully navigate this dual responsibility will not only thrive in the AI revolution of marketing but will set the standard for a future where personalization and privacy coexist harmoniously.

Building Trust in an AI-Driven World

As artificial intelligence weaves itself into the marketing tapestry, trust becomes the cornerstone upon which customer relationships are built. Trust, often conceived as a human attribute, now extends to the realms where data and machine learning touch every aspect of the consumer journey. Indeed, the rapid integration of AI within marketing strategies poses new challenges, but it also offers profound opportunities to foster trust at an unprecedented scale.

Firstly, let's acknowledge that trust is a multilayered concept in marketing, particularly when it involves AI. To cultivate trust, businesses must ensure their AI systems are reliable, transparent, and fair. Reliability means that the AI consistently performs as expected, minimizing errors that could damage customer relationships. Transparency involves openly sharing how AI systems work, what data they use, and how privacy is safeguarded. Fairness dictates that outcomes from AI should not be biased and should serve all sections of the audience impartially.

Transparency is critical in gaining trust. Marketers should strive to demystify AI technologies for their audience, explaining in simple terms how algorithms make decisions. This involves revealing the types of data collected, the purpose of its collection, and how it informs the AI's decision-making processes. It's about striking a balance between technical detail and accessibility. By opening up the 'black box' of AI, businesses can alleviate fears and build an informed trust amongst users.

Moreover, ethical considerations of AI deployments can't be overstressed. Respecting and protecting user privacy is paramount. This encompasses not only complying with regulations like GDPR or CCPA but exceeding them by adopting privacy by design principles in every AI system deployed. Marketers should advocate for customers' rights to their own data, providing clear options for consent and data withdrawal. Ethically aligned AI fosters trust through a commitment to do right by the customer beyond mere compliance.

In a world where AI impacts customer interactions, empathy doesn't lose its human touch—it evolves. Marketers can harness AI to understand customer emotions, needs, and reactions in real-time. However, integrating empathy effectively means ensuring AI interactions are not invasive but are contextually sensitive and appropriate. A trusted AI understands when to engage and when to step back, always prioritizing the customer's emotional experience.

Equitable AI, designed to eliminate bias, is also a fundamental aspect of building trust. Diverse datasets and continuous algorithmic auditing are crucial to prevent AI from perpetuating stereotypes or unfairness. Marketers should work hand in hand with data scientists to routinely check for biases and ensure their AI systems treat all customers equitably. Diverse teams contribute to a diverse AI, which in turn can realistically cater to a global and diverse customer base.

Education and reassurance play a vital role as well. Educating customers about the benefits of AI, highlighting its convenience, personalized experiences, and seamless services can transform skepticism into advocacy. Reassurances through certifications, customer testimonials about AI's positive role, and proof of stringent security measures can fortify trust over time.

Additionally, accountability is non-negotiable. AI might run autonomously, but organizations must take full accountability for their systems' actions. This includes having clear policies for correcting mistakes and compensating customers when needed. An accountable organization doesn't shirk responsibility—it embraces the opportunity to improve and align AI more closely with human values.

One way to concrete trust is the continuous engagement with stakeholders. Throughout the lifecycle of AI systems, marketers should actively seek feedback from all users—external and internal. This feedback loop helps to refine AI tools and align their functionality with user expectations and societal norms. Listening becomes a powerful tool in the trust-building arsenal.

Moreover, AI should not only respect the present but also be future-proof. This means systems need to be designed to adapt to the changing expectations and norms of society. Marking foresight as a priority assures customers that they are not dealing with static, uncaring technology, but with a dynamic system that grows and improves with them.

When it comes to trust, consistency across all AI interactions is paramount. Whether it's chatbots, recommendation engines, or predictive analytics, the tone and responses should be coherent and reflect the brand's values. Inconsistency can be jarring and break the trust that might have taken years to build. This consistency should also extend to confronting and rectifying AI malfunctions or misunderstandings immediately.

Furthermore, recognizing the importance of human oversight is crucial in an AI-driven world. While AI can manage many tasks, the human element cannot be replaced—especially in complex or sensitive situations. There should always be an easy way for customers to escalate an issue from AI to a human who can understand and address their concerns more deeply.

Lastly, patience in the trust-building process is essential. Trust isn't won overnight, especially with something as complex as AI. Marketers must be prepared for a marathon, not a sprint, continually demonstrating the value and safety of AI-enhanced interactions over time.

In summary, fostering trust in an AI-driven world is not just about deploying cutting-edge technology—it's about placing humanity at the core of digital transformation. By focusing on reliability, transparency, fairness, education, accountability, engagement, future-proofing, consistency, human oversight, and above all, patience, marketers can build a strong, trusting relationship with their audience. It's this trust that will empower customers to embrace the AI revolution, unlocking the full potential of AI in global marketing strategies.

Marketers, innovators, and strategists now have the opportunity to lead this charge, to guide AI developments with a principled approach that prioritizes human values. The coming chapters will delve deeper into the practical implications, strategies, and tools available for achieving this delicate balance in various facets of marketing. The integrity of the AI systems we build, and the trust they instill, will be the defining factors of success in the AI-enhanced world ahead.

Regulatory Compliance and AI

In exploring the labyrinthine junctures where artificial intelligence intersects with global marketing, we're compelled to address a vital component: regulatory compliance. The ubiquitous deployment of AI in digital marketing strategies has necessitated an in-depth understanding of the regulatory frameworks that govern their use. As marketers, navigating the shoals of compliance while leveraging AI's transformative potential is as crucial as the innovations themselves.

Firstly, let us acknowledge that the legal landscape for AI is a patchwork of regional and international regulations. This is compounded by the pace at which AI evolves, often outstripping the legal frameworks designed to regulate it. Businesses must remain agile, adapting to legislative changes to avoid punitive repercussions and to maintain consumer trust.

At the heart of AI regulatory compliance lies data protection and privacy laws. The General Data Protection Regulation (GDPR) in the European Union, for instance, sets stringent rules on data handling and user consent, implications of which ripple globally. As AI systems are fueled by data, staying abreast of such privacy regulations is indispensable.

Furthermore, the landscape of compliance extends beyond data protection to include specific AI governance policies. These are designed to ensure that AI systems operate transparently, without bias, and in a manner that does not harm users. For marketers, this means ensuring the AI tools they deploy are compliant with ethical standards, accentuating the need for ethical AI design and use.

Another critical aspect of regulatory compliance is algorithmic transparency. Marketing strategies that utilize AI must be able to explain how decisions are made, particularly when they affect consumer experiences and choices. This transparency extends to include the reasoning behind targeted advertisements or personalized recommendations.

Marketing professionals must also consider the interpretability of their AI systems. Not only should these systems comply with the letter of the law, but also its spirit. The objective isn't simply to avoid legal action but to foster trust among consumers who are growing increasingly conscious about how their data is used.

Let's turn our focus to industry-specific regulations that impact the use of AI in marketing. For instance, financial services have stringent compliance mandates that regulate the use of AI in marketing related to investments, credit, and insurance. Every sector, from healthcare to entertainment, has unique regulatory challenges that marketers must understand and respect.

Moreover, marketers should anticipate the evolution of AI policy as technology and societal norms change. A future-proof strategy is one that not only meets current compliance needs but also adapts to upcoming regulations. The most forward-thinking organizations participate in policy discussions and development, influencing the future regulatory environment in which they'll operate.

In the context of global marketing, compliance is even more complex. Marketers must be cognizant of the regulatory nuances in each geographical market they serve. The astute use of AI in marketing therefore demands not only technological prowess but also geopolitical awareness and agility.

Risk management is an integral part of compliance. Firms must conduct regular audits of their AI systems to ensure compliance with diverse and evolving regulations. Marketing teams must collaborate with legal and compliance departments to identify and mitigate potential risks posed by the AI technologies they deploy.

Training and development are indispensable in fostering a compliance-minded culture within a marketing team. Investing in continuous education about AI and its regulatory environment empowers marketers to make informed decisions and implement best practices consistently.

While there may be temptation to view compliance as a limitation to innovation, a different perspective is warranted. Compliance, when embraced, can serve as a strong foundation upon which trust is built with consumers. It's an opportunity to distinguish a brand as a responsible and ethical steward of AI.

Lastly, we must consider the implications of non-compliance. Failing to adhere to regulations can result in substantial fines, legal disputes, and irreparable damage to a brand's reputation. Marketers must recognize that compliance is not a mere box-ticking exercise, but a safeguard against these risks.

Regulatory compliance in the realm of AI and marketing is not merely a legal necessity—it's an ethical imperative and a strategic enabler. As we embrace the transformative power of AI, we must also commit to the responsible and compliant application of these powerful tools. It is this balanced approach that will help harness the full potential of AI in global marketing while maintaining the trust and confidence of consumers worldwide.

Chapter 10:
Global Marketing and Cross-Cultural AI Adaptation

Having explored the intricacies of AI in forging deeper customer relationships and ensuring privacy, it's imperative to pivot our focus towards the burgeoning global marketplace and the indispensable role of cross-cultural adaptation within AI-driven marketing strategies. Global marketing no longer thrives on a one-size-fits-all approach; it demands that AI technologies are not merely exported, but intricately woven into the cultural fabric of each unique market. In this strategic synthesis, we delve into tailoring AI applications to navigate the complexities of local customs, languages, and consumer behaviors, ensuring that global branding remains consistent yet sensitive to regional nuances. Marketers are tasked with the sophisticated choreography of global campaigns that resonate locally, powered by AI tools adept at deciphering and adapting to the subtleties of cultural diversity. It is in this space that we uncover the true agility of AI—its potential to be a linchpin for marketing campaigns that are as locally authentic as they are globally expansive.

Localizing AI Strategies for Global Markets

One cannot overstate the importance of localizing AI strategies to fit the diverse tapestry of global markets. As businesses scale into new regions, an understanding of cultural nuances alongside employing region-specific AI applications is crucial to ensure effective engagement with local audiences. AI, with its vast computational powers, provides a remarkable tool for such customization. However, without a clear strategy for localization, companies risk alienating potential consumers and missing out on key opportunities for growth.

For local markets to fully embrace global brands, a sense of familiarity and relevance must be established. This begins with localized language and dialects, where AI's natural language processing abilities can adapt messaging and content. A brand speaking in the local tongue, both literally and figuratively, resonates more profoundly, demonstrating respect and understanding of cultural contexts. Brands that achieve this earn a place in the day-to-day lives of local consumers.

Predictive analytics aid in interpreting the trends and preferences within different cultural contexts. When AI is tuned to discern local patterns, it can predict shifts in consumer behavior with uncanny accuracy. This is particularly valuable in fast-changing markets where traditional research methods may struggle to keep up. Predictive analytics can flag up-and-coming trends, allowing marketers to align their strategies accordingly.

Automation can be localized too. Look at programmatic advertising - AI can optimize ad placements by analyzing data on where ads perform best within each market, giving consideration to local regulatory norms, cultural preferences, and media consumption habits. By weaving local preferences into the AI's learning algorithm, advertising becomes not only targeted but also culturally adapted.

It's also important not to underestimate the role that AI can play in social media as it bridges the gap between global brands and local markets. With AI tools, marketers can automate and localize social media content promptly, responding to social cues and dialogues specific to each locale. Social listening AI tools can track local conversations, slang, and trending topics, ensuring the brand's content is universally accepted yet locally engaging.

The consumer journey, too, is subject to regional variations. AI's capability in customer journey mapping has to account for these differences to be effective. With AI-powered analytics, businesses can tailor online experiences, considering the unique online shopping behaviors seen in different cultures. This may range from payment preferences to the approach to customer service, with virtual assistants programmed to understand local idioms and values.

Search algorithms are another key area that must be localized. Understanding how local markets use search engines can empower AI to optimize for regional search trends, language use, and preferred types of content. The difference between optimizing for Google versus Baidu, for instance, is not just a technical question but a deep cultural one, affecting everything from keyword selection to website design.

AI also has profound implications for the e-commerce landscape. As businesses work to provide customized shopping experiences, localization goes beyond translating language; it involves customizing AI algorithms to understand local buying patterns, festival seasons, and even the impact of local weather on consumer preferences. Inventory and supply chain management AI systems can anticipate demand surges during local holidays and adjust stock levels accordingly, averting stockouts or overstock situations.

With global expansion comes the challenge of maintaining data privacy and building trust. In differing markets, the societal perception of AI's use in personalization and data collection can vary dramatically. Here, localizing AI strategies means adapting to the local regulatory and ethical landscape—understanding that what's acceptable in one country may be frowned upon or even illegal in another.

Entering global markets also offers an opportunity for multinational brands to embrace cultural sensitivity in AI applications. This not only means avoiding faux pas but also harnessing cultural insights to elevate brand positioning and build genuinely meaningful connections. Localization is not about losing global brand identity—it's about adapting it in a way that shows attentiveness and care towards the consumer's cultural surroundings.

It's essential for businesses looking to globalize to foster local teams that possess an intricate knowledge of the regional market and can work in tandem with AI technologies. These teams can ensure the AI's outputs are appropriately localized, be it for a marketing campaign, chatbot interactions, or predictive market analyses. They act as the cultural lens through which AI insights must be interpreted and, if necessary, corrected.

Adapting strategies for global markets doesn't mean compromising on brand consistency. AI can help manage global branding by ensuring message and visual consistency across languages and cultures, while still permitting for local adaptations that resonate with each specific audience. An AI system trained with the brand's core values and visual standards will uphold the integrity of the brand while making the necessary contextual adjustments.

In meeting the demand for local relevance, there's a treasure trove of opportunities for businesses to create deep, long-lasting consumer connections through nuanced, culturally intelligent AI strategies. While global expansion may seem like a homogenizing force, it's the localized AI strategies that truly allow a brand to sing in harmony with the rich, diverse backgrounds of the global marketplace. Such an approach acknowledges that beneath the data and algorithms, the heart of global marketing is human connection—deeply personal and proudly diverse.

Finally, it's valuable to step back and consider the panoramic view of what localizing AI for global markets embodies. It's not solely a technological undertaking, but a strategic one that loops in the cultural, ethical, and human elements. It's a blend of science and art, where marketers leverage cutting-edge technology to grasp and adapt to the cultural fabric within which their brand will thrive. In doing so, companies can not only gain competitive advantage but also play a part in fostering cross-cultural understanding and appreciation, ultimately driving global innovation in an AI-augmented reality.

The pursuit of localizing AI for global markets is a testament to the boundless potential AI holds when strategically infused with human insight and sensitivity. For marketers aspiring to tap into this potential, localizing AI is not just an option; it's a strategic imperative that defines the successful integration of AI into the heart of global market strategies.

Cultural Sensitivity in AI Applications

When marketing transcends borders, it's imperative that strategies are adapted and nuanced enough to resonate with diverse global audiences. AI, the great enabler in this realm, carries with it an immense responsibility: to ensure that messaging, content, and interaction are culturally sensitive and contextually appropriate. This section plunges into the heart of cultural sensitivity as it's woven into the fabric of AI applications in marketing.

At its core, cultural sensitivity is the understanding and respect for cultural differences, including language, customs, beliefs, and norms. In global marketing, lack of cultural sensitivity can result in campaigns that are, at best, ineffective and, at worst, offensive. AI, with its data-driven insights and precision, can be an ally in navigating these complexities—if programmed with diversity in mind.

As marketers, the use of AI in campaigns must be preceded by a thorough analysis of the target culture. This includes understanding colloquialisms that may not translate well, local customs that could influence purchasing decisions, and even color symbolism that differs from one culture to another. The adoption of such AI requires more than technical prowess; it demands cultural empathy and an ongoing learning process.

Algorithm bias is a pressing issue when it comes to cultural sensitivity. Developers often encode their unconscious biases into AI, which can reinforce stereotypes and perpetuate inequalities. To combat this, there is a strong need for diverse teams that work on AI programs, ensuring a variety of perspectives influence the design and implementation phase of these intelligent systems.

Artificial intelligence can be programmed to perform sentiment analysis on a large scale. But herein lies the nuanced challenge: sentiments are not universally expressed similarly. For instance, direct communication is valued in some cultures, whereas others prefer a more indirect approach. An AI that fails to grasp these subtleties could misinterpret social cues and sentiments, potentially alienating the very audience it's trying to engage.

One critical application of AI in addressing cultural sensitivity is through personalization. A keen AI system can tailor experiences to individuals based on cultural context. This capability, however, must be finely tuned to avoid over-generalization. It's not enough to lump all individuals from a region into a homogenous group; careful segmentation and nuanced customization are key.

Localized content is another domain where AI shines with proper guidance. Efficiently scaling marketing content to diverse regions is challenging, yet a culturally tuned AI can manage this by adapting text, images, and references to be locally relevant. This fosters a sense of connection with the brand, showing respect for the consumer's cultural background and potentially boosting engagement and conversion rates.

Customer support and chatbots represent another frontier where cultural sensitivity is paramount. These AI-powered interfaces often serve as the first point of contact for consumers. They must be meticulously crafted to understand and respond appropriately to cultural cues, whether in language subtleties or in understanding the local context of inquiries or complaints.

A not-so-obvious application of AI in ensuring cultural sensitivity is in product recommendations. While recommendations are often based on past behavior, incorporating cultural intelligence can lead to more respectful and appropriate suggestions. Consider festivities unique to a culture when recommending products or avoiding gifting taboos that might offend the recipient.

Data collection and analysis through AI also tread a careful path around cultural sensitivities. With varying degrees of acceptability around personal data usage, AI systems must be attuned to what's considered private or intrusive in different cultures. Failure to recognize these boundaries could not only spell trouble with local regulations but can damage brand trust irreparably.

In global marketing campaigns, AI has the incredible ability to adapt messaging in real-time across various platforms. This dynamic approach is potent when combined with cultural sensitivity, allowing for rapid adjustments to marketing material that may not be resonating—or worse, is received negatively by the target audience.

Ultimately, the effectiveness of AI in cultural sensitivity is a reflection of the data it's fed. Rich, diverse datasets lead to more accurately reflective AI behavior. This underlines the importance of data collection strategies that prioritize diversity, ensuring a multiplicity of cultural backgrounds is considered when training AI systems.

Translation is an essential operation where AI is heavily employed. While AI translators have become more sophisticated, subtleties, especially idiomatic expressions and cultural references, often get lost. Therefore, integrating human checks into the AI translation process ensures that translations aren't just linguistically correct but are culturally nuanced and sensitive as well.

Leveraging the power of AI to foster inclusivity can also set a brand apart. An AI that's programmed to recognize and celebrate cultural differences through campaigns that spotlight diversity can resonate deeply with consumers. It demonstrates a brand's commitment to inclusivity and can strengthen a brand's position within a multicultural marketplace.

In conclusion, cultural sensitivity in AI applications isn't just about programming a machine to recognize patterns; it's about embedding a deep understanding of and respect for human diversity into the heart of marketing efforts. Done well, AI can offer a nuanced edge in crafting campaigns that are not only effective but are met with nods of appreciation from culturally rich and varied audiences the world over.

As global marketing marches forward, AI stands at the ready, poised to bridge linguistic and cultural divides. Its careful application promises not just business intelligence but a form of cultural compassion, tuned carefully by the human intellect and empathy that guide its algorithms. Wherever this dynamic nexus of technology and cultural sensitivity leads, it promises to redefine the very fabric of global marketing strategy and practice.

Managing Global Brand Consistency with AI

As the world flattens into a global marketplace, the challenge to maintain brand consistency across borders intensifies. Marketers are now entrusted with the daunting task of ensuring that a brand's essence, its values, and its promise remain unaltered no matter where it appears. This consistency is vital as it underpins the trust and recognition that customers place in a brand. Artificial intelligence offers novel and compelling methodologies to uphold this consistency in ways that are both scalable and adaptive.

Harnessing the power of AI for brand consistency begins with understanding the data-driven nature of branding. AI systems can analyze customer interactions, preferences, and feedback across different markets to ensure a brand's message resonates universally yet remains sensitive to local nuances. Through advanced algorithms, AI can detect and harmonize discrepancies that may arise in branding materials across different countries.

One of the foundational elements of global brand management is monitoring. With AI, the task of monitoring becomes less arduous. AI-powered tools can systematically scan through online content, examining social media, websites, and advertisements to verify that brand guidelines are adhered to globally. This constant vigilance helps identify inconsistencies quickly, often in real-time, allowing for immediate course correction.

Content creation, too, can be revolutionized by AI. As brands look to speak to a global audience, AI's natural language processing capabilities enable the mass production of content that is both locally relevant and consistent with the brand's core message. This means promotional materials, social media posts, and other marketing communications can be tailored for distinct markets without losing the overarching brand narrative.

Language is often a formidable barrier in maintaining brand consistency. Fortunately, AI-driven translation services go beyond literal word-for-word translation. They encompass the subtleties of local idioms and cultural contexts to maintain the intended impact of marketing messages. When a brand's message travels across linguistic borders, it's crucial that the essence of what is communicated remains intact. AI's sophisticated language models are instrumental in achieving this delicate balance.

Consistency in brand imagery is as crucial as the messaging itself. AI's image recognition and processing capabilities enable brands to maintain a consistent visual identity across diverse markets. This tech ensures that visuals align with brand standards by evaluating colors, logos, and the overall aesthetic of marketing assets—equating to a universally cohesive brand image.

Another significant aspect of brand management is customer engagement. AI can personalize interactions without deviating from the brand's voice or values. Whether it's through chatbots, emails, or other communication channels, each customer interaction can be both personalized and consistent with the brand, managed at scale across the globe.

For legal and ethical compliance, AI's capability to understand and adapt to various regulatory environments is invaluable. It ensures that marketing activities not only align with the brand's standards but also with local laws and cultural expectations, mitigating the risk of costly missteps.

Feedback loops are critical in brand management. AI analytics empower brands to collect, analyze, and act on customer feedback across different regions efficiently. By understanding sentiments across markets, businesses can adjust strategies to maintain a cohesive brand experience. This constant adaptation within a framework of consistency is what sets apart successful global brands.

In implementing AI for global brand consistency, it's essential to recognize that technology is a means to an end, not the end itself. The goal is to amplify the brand's reach while maintaining its core identity. AI aids in achieving the ubiquity of a brand while preserving its uniqueness. Marketers must therefore maintain stewardship over AI strategies, guiding them with human insights and creativity.

On the operational side, AI-driven automation of brand management tasks frees up human resources to focus on strategy and creative endeavors. This allows marketing teams to concentrate on building brand equity rather than getting bogged down by the minutiae of consistency checks.

Adapting to market changes is another arena where AI shines. With predictive analytics, AI can forecast shifts in consumer behavior or market dynamics, prompting proactive adjustments in branding efforts. This foresight ensures brands remain consistent yet dynamic, evolving with the marketplace.

The integration of AI in managing global brand consistency can also be a unifying force for marketing teams spread throughout the world. Shared AI platforms foster cohesion and collaboration among team members, regardless of location, centralizing brand efforts and messaging.

Finally, AI's influence on data security cannot be overlooked. As brands gather and utilize vast amounts of data, keeping this information safe is paramount. AI's advanced security protocols and anomaly detection systems work to protect brand and customer data, a non-negotiable aspect of maintaining brand integrity.

In an era where brands transcend geographic and digital boundaries, AI offers the needed scalability and sophistication to cultivate and maintain global brand consistency. However, the technology should be employed with a sense of purpose and direction guided by seasoned marketers who understand the delicate interplay between global appeal and local relevance—both of which shape the modern consumer's brand expectations. By maintaining this balance, marketers can leverage AI to forge brands that are not only consistent on the global stage but also deeply resonant with customers from every corner of the world.

Chapter 11:
AI Talent and Skills for Marketers

Moving seamlessly from the global kaleidoscope of cross-cultural AI applications in marketing, we now turn our focus inward to the core competencies and the intellectual might that modern marketers must wield: AI talent and skills essential for a revolutionized marketing landscape. A new arsenal of skills has become indispensable, where marketers aren't just creatives with a knack for consumer psychology but also astute technologists who navigate data, algorithms, and machine learning with as much ease as they do market trends. Embracing AI requires a fundamental reinvention of the marketer's skill set, making continuous education and agile learning frameworks the bedrock for success. From understanding the nuances of data-driven decision-making to spearheading innovative customer experiences powered by AI, marketers are the new hybrid professionals. They're expected to have a foot in the analytical world of machines and another in the human realm of storytelling and relationship-building. Developing this duality of competence within marketing teams becomes a pivotal task for leadership. This chapter delves into creating an environment where marketing professionals are empowered to grow into their roles as AI-savvy strategists, driving change, and fostering a culture that's both data-literate and creatively charged, preparing for a future where AI is not just a tool but a co-creator in the marketing narrative.

The New Marketing Skill Set

As we delve deeper into the intricacies of AI in global marketing, it becomes paramount to discuss the evolution of the marketer's toolkit. Today's marketers can no longer rely solely on traditional strategies and methods; they must embrace a new set of skills tailored for the AI revolution. This skill set calls for a harmonious blend of technical prowess, strategic insight, creative thinking, and an empathetic understanding of consumer behavior.

The first of these indispensable abilities is proficiency in data analytics. Marketers must feel at home amidst vast quantities of data, discerning patterns and extracting actionable insights. They must be capable of working with AI tools that handle predictive analytics, understanding not only how to interpret the data but also how to apply it effectively in crafting personalized experiences for customers.

Secondly, an understanding of machine learning and its applications in marketing is critical. A marketer with skills in this domain can supervise AI algorithms as they optimize campaigns and refine content strategies. It's about recognizing the power of AI to predict trends, customize content, and automate tasks, but it's also about overseeing these processes to ensure they align with brand values and customer expectations.

Thirdly, creative skills remain invaluable; however, they now must be exercised in concert with AI tools. Marketers should be able to use AI-driven programs to enhance their creative output, whether through content curation, ad targeting, or real-time personalizations. This involves a mixture of artistic sense and an innovative mindset, staying abridged of how AI can complement and augment the creative process.

Technical aptitude is another piece of the puzzle. Marketers don't need to become expert coders, but a working knowledge of how AI technologies function can greatly enhance their ability to collaborate with data scientists and engineers. This allows for a clearer communication channel when deploying new AI tools or troubleshooting existing systems.

Emotional intelligence comes hand-in-hand with technological skill. The ability to empathize with the customer, understand their needs and desires, and predict how they might react to personalized content or automated support is a cornerstone of AI-driven marketing. This EQ helps ensure that despite the heavy lifting by machines, the human element in commerce remains at the forefront.

Strategic thinking in the age of AI warrants a novel approach. Marketers need to design strategies that integrate AI capabilities from the ground up, rather than retrofitting these technologies into existing plans. This requires vision—seeing the potential of AI to redefine market segments, customer service, and even the product offerings themselves.

Adaptability in this constantly evolving landscape is not just preferable; it's essential. Marketers must be agile learners, ready to adopt new AI technologies and strategies as they become available, and willing to abandon or iterate on tactics that no longer serve their purpose.

Change management expertise becomes more relevant as AI transforms marketing departments. Adept marketers will lead their teams through transitions, championing the adoption of AI while mitigating fears and resistance to change. They serve as the bridge between the human and digital elements of the organization.

Finally, the skill set for AI-driven marketers includes an adherence to ethical standards and practices. As the custodians of consumer data and the executors of AI algorithms, marketers must navigate the fine line between personalization and privacy, ensuring their actions foster trust and comply with regulations.

Continual learning is also part of this new marketing skill set. Marketers ought to stay abreast of emerging technologies and theoretical knowledge in AI, ensuring they can recognize and seize new opportunities as they arise. Lifelong education in this domain is no longer an option but a requisite for sustained success.

Collaboration skills are also vital, as AI-driven marketing is seldom a solo endeavor. It requires harmony between various departments, external partners, and often across borders. Marketers must be able to work within diverse teams, leveraging the strengths of each member to realize a cohesive AI integration.

The next generation of marketers is also expected to be both generalists and specialists. A broad understanding of multiple marketing facets ensures a seamless integration of AI strategies, while a deep dive into specific areas like SEO, content creation, or customer experience provides a competitive edge.

Digital fluency, above all, must be woven into the marketer's fabric. This doesn't simply imply comfort with digital tools or platforms but extends to an innate ability to think in digital terms, applying this mindset to all facets of marketing strategy and execution.

Lastly, resilience in the face of failure is a skill that must be honed. The path to AI mastery in marketing is fraught with challenges and setbacks. Markers must learn to see failures as stepping stones, using them to build more robust and intelligent strategies.

In conclusion, the new skill set for marketers is diverse and dynamic, mirroring the multifaceted nature of AI itself. It includes a blend of hard and soft skills—ranging from data analysis to emotional intelligence, technical understanding to creative exploration. As we contemplate these competencies, we must always remember that AI serves to complement the marketer's role, not to replace it, strengthening the connection between brands and the global audience they serve.

Building AI Competence within Marketing Teams

As we venture further into the technologically driven marketing landscape, the intersection of AI and marketing becomes increasingly integral to strategic success. Marketers are at the forefront of this revolution, and to stay at the cutting edge, building AI competence within marketing teams is not just advised; it's imperative.

At the core of integrating AI into marketing lies the need for teams who are adept at navigating new tools and concepts. A marketer's acumen must now include an understanding of data analytics, machine learning, and the nuances of AI-driven strategies. Let's delve into cultivating this expertise within your marketing team to ensure they are well-equipped for the shifts in the industry.

To start, the foundational step is education. Continuous learning environments are crucial for marketing teams. Short courses, workshops, and webinars on AI and its applications in marketing can help bridge the knowledge gap. This learning should cover algorithmic principles, data analysis, and ethical considerations, to name a few areas.

Hiring for AI competence is another strategy. When recruiting new talent, prioritize candidates with backgrounds in data science, machine learning, or AI. These individuals can serve as catalysts for change within your organization, infusing their know-how into every campaign and strategy discussion.

Encouraging cross-functional collaboration is also vital. Integrate AI specialists with marketing veterans to foster a culture of mutual learning and innovation. Collaboration leads to fusion of traditional marketing strategies with cutting-edge AI tactics, a hybrid that can yield genuinely transformative results.

Alongside collaboration, promoting an experimental mindset is key. AI is rapidly evolving, and marketing solutions that are revolutionary today may become outdated tomorrow. Encourage teams to test new approaches, learn from failures, and innovate continuously.

Digital savvy within teams should extend beyond traditional marketing tools. Invest in AI-powered tools for customer relationship management, content creation, data analysis, and other functions. Ensure that team members not only have access to these tools but are also proficient in using them.

Implement mentorship programs to cultivate in-house expertise. Experienced marketers can take under their wing less AI-savvy colleagues, gradually bringing them up to speed with one-on-one training and mentorship on AI applications in marketing.

Develop a centralized knowledge base where learnings and resources can be stored. This ensures that insights gained from AI experiments and campaigns are not lost but are used to inform future strategies and educate team members.

Real-world application should go hand-in-hand with theoretical understanding. Encourage teams to apply AI insights to live projects, enabling them to see the impact of AI-driven decisions in real-time and adjust tactics accordingly.

Don't overlook the role of leadership in championing AI competence. Leadership must communicate the value of AI in marketing, set clear objectives for AI integration, and allocate resources for training and development initiatives.

Adopt a culture that rewards ingenuity. As marketers experiment with AI, celebrate their successes and recognize intelligent risk-taking, even if it doesn't always lead to immediate success. This attitude helps to create a safe space for innovation, crucial in a field as dynamic as AI.

It's imperative too, to focus on ethics and trust. With AI tapping into vast amounts of consumer data, teams must understand the responsibilities that come with it. Training on ethical AI use and its implications on privacy and consumer trust is necessary for maintaining a brand's integrity.

Finally, integrate AI competency development into performance reviews and career progression pathways. By doing so, marketers are incentivized to develop their skills and contribute to the AI-driven goals of the organization.

To conclude, building AI competence within marketing teams isn't solely about hiring experts or attending training sessions. It's about creating a culture that values continuous learning, supports innovation, and champions collaboration. It's a culture where AI isn't just a tool but a transformative force shaping the very essence of global marketing strategies. As AI continues to redefine the future of marketing, those teams that embed AI into their DNA will not only remain competitive but also set the pace for an industry in constant evolution.

In the coming sections, we'll explore further how leadership can foster this environment and the new marketing skill set needed to thrive in an AI-enhanced world. Look forward to a synthesis of strategy, insight, and foresight - elements that define future-ready marketing teams in the AI era.

Leadership in AI-Enhanced Marketing

The vanguard of innovation in marketing today is not merely steeped in creativity and traditional acumen, but also in the burgeoning domain of artificial intelligence. Leaders in this space must foster an environment where AI can thrive alongside human insight, forming a symbiotic relationship that propels marketing strategies into new frontiers of effectiveness and personalization.

The transformative journey of integrating AI into the marketing toolkit requires more than just the adoption of technology; it calls for a visionary approach. Leadership in AI-enhanced marketing demands an amalgamation of technical fluency with strategic foresight. Market leaders are expected to not only discern the potential of AI but to navigate the complex moral and ethical landscape that accompanies its use. The stewardship of customer data and the maintenance of privacy must be judiciously balanced against the quest for hyper-personalization and efficiency.

Creating a culture of innovation within an organization is pivotal. This involves encouraging a mindset of continuous learning and adaptation. Marketing leaders must foster teams that are agile, highly skilled, and open to the exchange of ideas. An environment where experimentation is valued, even if it leads to occasional failure, is essential for the evolution of AI-enhanced marketing strategies.

In this digital realm, mentors and visionaries must also underscore the importance of collaboration between machines and humans. While AI can provide invaluable insights through data analysis and pattern recognition, the creative and empathetic aspects of marketing remain quintessentially human. Celebrating this partnership is crucial to crafting campaigns that resonate deeply with the audience.

A critical aspect of leadership is steering the ethical compass of AI applications in marketing. Transparency in how AI algorithms derive insights, make decisions, and learn from data is vital to harness trust from both customers and team members alike. Leaders ought to advocate for processes that are not only legally compliant but also align with the broader values of the society in which they operate.

Preparation for an AI-driven future begins with the cultivation of talent. Progressive leaders must prioritize the development of AI skills within their marketing teams. This involves not only technical upskilling but also instilling an analytics mindset across the organization. Integration of AI training programs can arm marketers with the necessary competencies to leverage AI tools effectively.

At the heart of AI-enhanced marketing is the ability to anticipate customer needs. Leaders who exercise foresight in deploying predictive analytics can gain a competitive edge. They can preempt market shifts and consumer trends by harnessing the predictive capabilities offered by AI, delivering a proactive approach to market demands rather than being reactive.

Furthermore, leadership in this sphere necessitates a discerning approach to vendor selection and technology investments. Marketers must be judicious in choosing partners that align with their strategic vision and can provide scalable AI solutions. Vetting potential AI tools and platforms for their reliability, security, and their ability to integrate smoothly into existing systems is a nuanced skill that leaders must possess.

Executing AI-enhanced marketing strategies also means being a champion of change management. Leaders need to guide their teams through the transformation that AI brings, managing resistance and the natural human apprehension towards AI. The goal is to underline the opportunities that AI presents, not just for the business, but also for personal and professional growth.

One must not overlook the global aspect of AI in marketing—understanding and adapting AI applications to different cultures and markets is paramount. Leaders who command a global perspective can prevent the homogenization of marketing efforts and ensure that AI creates culturally resonant content, tailored to the nuances of regional markets.

Monitoring the landscape of AI in marketing is a continuous process. The innovation cycle in this field is rapid, and being at the helm means staying informed about the latest developments. Leaders should engage with industry forums, participate in thought leadership, and contribute to the collective knowledge base of AI in marketing.

Conclusively, leaders in AI-enhanced marketing are the orchestrators of a complex symphony that intermingles technology, human ingenuity, and ethics. They are not just implementers of AI, but the guardians of the brand-customer relationship in an increasingly digital world. Their role is pivotal in ensuring that AI serves to augment human creativity, foster meaningful connections with consumers, and elevates the brand in a rapily changing marketing landscape.

In the spirit of innovation, leaders are also tasked with showcasing the successes and learning from the setbacks of AI deployments. Openly sharing these experiences paves the way for industry-wide improvement and sets the stage for ongoing refinement of AI in marketing strategies.

In closing, the mantle of leadership in AI-enhanced marketing is a dynamic and ever-evolving one. It's an exciting ascent that requires a blend of courage, curiosity, and commitment to ethical practices. Those at the forefront will not only transform their brands but also shape the future landscape of global marketing.

Chapter 12:
Innovating with AI: Case Studies
of Success and Failure

Continuing our exploration into the transformative power of AI within the marketing domain, Chapter 12 delves into a riveting analysis of concrete examples spanning diverse industries. We learn from decorated successes where AI integration not only revamped marketing efforts, but also forged unprecedented customer relationships, catalyzing a surge in both satisfaction and profitability. Likewise, we investigate instances where AI's promises fell short, deconstructing failures to uncover crucial lessons. Through these lessons, marketers are equipped with the distilled wisdom necessary for harnessing AI's potential while thoughtfully navigating its complexities. This chapter isn't just about the tales of triumph and caution; it's a treasure trove of strategic insights that facilitate innovative problem-solving and the cultivation of resilient marketing strategies resilient in the face of AI's constant evolution.

Learning from Real-World AI Implementations

As modern marketers, it's vital not only to envision AI's potential but to ground our strategies in the reality of its applications. Exploring real-world cases where AI has been implemented allows us to navigate through the complexities of technology-driven marketing strategies with a keener sense of what works, what doesn't, and what it takes to succeed in this rapidly evolving landscape.

Every forward-thinking business today needs a compass to navigate the AI terrain. Case studies of AI in marketing not only serve this purpose but also present a treasure trove of lessons. They help us discern patterns of success, common obstacles, and innovative strategies that break new ground. Analyzing such cases can reveal insights that go beyond theoretical knowledge, making the difference between thriving and simply surviving in the digital marketplace.

Leverage AI to understand consumer behavior, for instance, has gone from speculative to demonstrative. Brands that have mastered predictive analytics are able to tailor their marketing efforts in unparalleled ways, achieving personalization at a scale which seemed impossible just a few years ago. Witnessing these examples first-hand prompts a reflective pause to consider how our own strategies could evolve.

AI-driven content creation and curation, as another example, has revolutionized the way brands communicate with their audience. Real-world successes in this domain showcase AI's ability to produce engaging, relevant content swiftly, aligning with consumer interests and behaviors while freeing human creatives to focus on strategy and nuanced brand narratives.

Programmatic advertising harnesses machine learning in a way that is transforming the marketing ecosystem. By studying real-world cases where companies have tapped into AI for ad targeting and optimization, marketers can gain insights into the mechanisms behind successful campaigns that balance reach, relevance, and ROI.

Social media strategies augmented by AI offer a glimpse into the future of digital engagement. From identifying trending topics to optimizing post timings, AI tools are arming marketers with the ability to act on real-time data. Examining successful implementations in this area not only inspires innovation but also equips marketers with the know-how to leverage AI for competitive advantage.

Diving deep into how businesses are using AI to bolster customer experience and support unveils layers of sophistication in modern customer interactions. Chatbots and virtual assistants that provide seamless support are no longer novelties but benchmarks of exceptional service. Analyzing these real-world implementations can teach us how to enhance brand loyalty and customer satisfaction through thoughtful AI integration.

E-commerce platforms leveraging AI offer a window into the future of online shopping. Real-world case studies in this sector highlight how AI is being used to predict trends, manage inventory, and provide personalized shopping experiences, all of which stand as invaluable lessons for marketers looking to excel in the digital domain.

When considering privacy and trust, real-world applications of AI in marketing present a cautionary tale. They delineate a delicate balance between leveraging data for personalization and maintaining consumer trust. Businesses that navigate these waters successfully illustrate strategies that preserve consumer rights while optimizing marketing effectiveness.

Another rich source of insight comes from examining how AI is adapted to various cultures in global marketing. Real-world cases show that localizing AI requires more than just translating content; it involves deep cultural understanding and tailoring strategies to resonate with local consumer behaviors and preferences.

Swiveling toward the human element, real-world cases around building AI talent within marketing teams emphasize the importance of cultivating a skill set that blends marketing savvy with technical acumen. Learning from the trenches, businesses are discovering efficient ways to upskill their teams and foster a culture of continuous learning.

Lastly, not all lessons stem from success. Failures in AI implementations carry potent learnings of their own. By studying what led to these missteps, whether it's overreliance on AI without human oversight or misjudging user privacy concerns, marketers can develop a keen eye for potential pitfalls and a proactive approach to avoid them.

As we progress through the tales of triumph and caution offered by real-world AI applications, key themes emerge that define the hallmark of successful AI implementation in marketing. These include a rigorous understanding of the technology, a clear vision for its role within the broader strategy, an ongoing commitment to experiment and learn, and a relentless focus on the customer's experience and value gained.

With these real-world implementations as our guide, we march forward, emboldened by the knowledge that AI is not just a disruptive force but also a transformative ally in the quest for marketing that resonates deeply and universally. The lessons gleaned from these implementations equip us as marketers to craft strategies that are not only data-driven but also deeply human in their orientation, acknowledging the intricate dance between technology and the timeless art of connecting with consumers.

Understanding the contours of success in AI-driven marketing through the lens of real-world implementations serves not just as a retrospective outlook but as a vital blueprint for the future. As we harness these insights, we prepare ourselves to write the next chapter of marketing innovation, where AI is woven into the very fabric of how brands interact, engage, and grow in a globalized, digital-first world.

Best Practices for AI in Marketing

In the grand mosaic of digital marketing, artificial intelligence (AI) has quickly become the golden thread that weaves efficiency, personalization, and deeper consumer insights into the fabric of marketing strategies. As marketers aim to harness the power of AI, it becomes essential to approach this technology with best practices that ensure effective, ethical, and sustainable results. These best practices not only fuel a competitive advantage but also pave the way for novel paradigms in customer engagement.

Understanding the scope of AI tools is the first tenet of best practice. Marketers must recognize that AI isn't a one-size-fits-all solution but rather a diverse set of technologies that range from machine learning algorithms to natural language processing. By grasping the capabilities and limitations of each application, one can develop a realistic and goal-oriented AI marketing strategy that is aligned with business objectives.

Data quality is another cornerstone. AI's output is only as good as the data inputted. Marketers should invest in data management and ensure that the AI systems they deploy are trained on high-quality, relevant, and diverse datasets. This diligence not only improves the accuracy of AI insights but also mitigates biases that can lead to flawed decision-making.

An ethically sound AI practice is paramount; it should be transparent and explainable to stakeholders and consumers alike. Marketing strategies must comply with evolving regulations and data privacy norms to foster trust and maintain brand integrity. It's not merely about using AI but using it responsibly.

Effective AI deployment in marketing also requires seamless integration into existing workflows. AI should complement human creativity and intuition rather than attempt to replace it. The synergy between marketers' expertise and AI's data-driven insights can lead to more robust and innovative campaigns.

Personalization is a buzzword that has been around in marketing circles for a long time. With AI, personalization can be executed at unprecedented scale. However, striking a balance between customized experiences and consumer privacy is increasingly critical. The best practices involve offering personalization that feels natural and relevant, rather than invasive or overwhelming.

Continuous learning and refinement is a part of AI's DNA and should be a part of its marketing applications. AI tools should not be set on autopilot; instead, they require ongoing evaluation and adjustment based on performance metrics and changing market dynamics. The agility to adapt strategies based on AI-generated insights can lead to improved outcomes over time.

AI systems tend to work in silos; integrating these systems to create a unified view of the customer journey is challenging yet crucial. This integration allows for a holistic approach to consumer interactions, ensuring that messages are coherent, timely, and effectively segmented across all touchpoints.

Looking beyond the obvious applications of AI in marketing to unlock innovative uses of technology can differentiate a brand. AI tools are continuously evolving, offering new opportunities such as image recognition, voice-based search, and sentiment analysis that can open untapped channels of consumer engagement.

Collaboration is key when it comes to AI. Marketers must work closely with data scientists, IT professionals, and other stakeholders to ensure that AI implementations are technically sound and aligned with the core marketing strategy. A collaborative environment fosters cross-functional learning and the sharing of insights, amplifying the effectiveness of AI capabilities.

Training and skill development form the backbone of AI adoption in marketing. Marketers need to develop a deep understanding of AI tools as well as maintain a culture of continual learning to keep pace with the rapidly changing landscape. Investing in education equips marketing teams to creatively leverage AI for optimal impact.

Testing and experimentation should be embedded into the AI adoption process. Marketers can't always predict how AI will influence consumer behavior, so it's essential to adopt an iterative approach that includes A/B testing, pilot programs, and feedback loops that inform strategy adjustments.

AI should be grounded in robust storytelling. Despite the power of data and automation, marketing remains fundamentally a story-driven discipline. The use of AI should enhance the storytelling capabilities of marketers, allowing for data-informed narratives that resonate deeply with target audiences.

To maximize AI's potential, one cannot overlook the importance of scalability. Marketing programs that utilize AI should be designed to scale up as the business grows, ensuring that the technology can handle increased loads and more complex decision-making without significant overhauls.

Finally, it is vital to maintain a future-focused mindset. The marketing landscape is in a perpetual state of evolution, influenced by new AI developments. Preparing for the future of AI in marketing means staying informed about emerging trends, adapting to new technologies, and being innovative in applying AI to solve marketing challenges.

Every AI application in marketing is an opportunity to learn, grow and refine strategies. By adhering to these best practices, marketers can navigate the AI terrain with confidence, harnessing its power to deliver exceptional value to businesses and customers alike. In an

AI-augmented marketing future, it's these practices that will empower brands to thrive and maintain relevance in a competitive global marketplace.

Avoiding Common Pitfalls

As we journey through the exploration of AI in global marketing, it's essential to recognize that while the opportunities are vast, so too are the potential pitfalls that can undermine the success of AI-driven initiatives. To maximize the effectiveness of AI in marketing, professionals need to be mindful of avoiding common errors that could stall progress and diminish returns. This section outlines various challenges to be vigilant of and provides strategies to circumvent these stumbling blocks, ensuring a seamless integration of AI into the marketing domain.

One frequently encountered pitfall is over-relying on AI without maintaining a balance with human intuition. While AI offers remarkable analytical capabilities, it's crucial for marketers not to discount the invaluable insights that human creativity and understanding bring to the table. A collaborative approach where AI augments human analysis, rather than replaces it, can provide better-rounded solutions that cater to the multifaceted nature of consumer behavior.

Another common oversight pertains to data dependency. AI systems thrive on large datasets, but this appetite for data can lead to concentrating on quantity over quality. Inaccurate, outdated, or biased data can result in poor decision-making. Marketers need to invest in data cleaning and validation processes to ensure the AI systems can generate accurate insights and recommendations.

Additionally, while personalized marketing is a powerful way to connect with customers, there's a fine line between personalization and invasion of privacy. Customer trust can be compromised if AI uses data in ways that customers find intrusive. Marketers need to establish clear guidelines for personalization, always prioritizing customer consent and transparency in data usage.

In the realm of programmatic advertising, a pitfall arises when marketers set and forget AI-driven campaigns. While AI can efficiently manage ad placements, human oversight is necessary to ensure that the strategies align with the overarching marketing goals and brand values. Regular audits and adjustments based on performance data are necessary to keep the campaigns relevant and effective.

For AI in social media, a potential misstep is not accounting for context in sentiment analysis. AI algorithms can struggle with nuances such as sarcasm and slang. Marketers need to combine AI tools with human judgment to accurately gauge public sentiment and avoid misinterpretation of online interactions.

Within customer support, the deployment of chatbots can lead to frustrations if they're not properly programmed to handle complex inquiries. The goal should be to enhance the customer experience with AI, not to create a barrier. Developing seamless hand-off protocols from AI to human agents can resolve this, providing customers with the support they need.

As search algorithms become more sophisticated, a pitfall is relying on outdated SEO practices. It's not enough to simply incorporate keywords. Marketers must understand the intricacies of semantic search and intent-based optimizations to ensure content remains discoverable and relevant to users' evolving search habits.

When it comes to e-commerce, the use of AI in personalization must be balanced. Over-personalization can lead to the "filter bubble" effect where customers are only exposed to a narrow set of products. Marketers should design AI systems that occasionally introduce unexpected products to encourage discovery and avoid limiting customer choice.

Privacy concerns form a significant pitfall in AI marketing. As regulatory compliance becomes more stringent, businesses must navigate the complexities of various data protection laws. It's vital to stay abreast of these regulations and to foster a company culture that respects customer privacy as a core value.

In targeting global markets, a pitfall can arise from a one-size-fits-all approach to AI implementation. Cultural nuances significantly impact consumer behavior, and AI systems need to be localized to reflect these differences. A deep understanding of local customs, languages, and preferences is crucial for AI marketing strategies to resonate with international audiences.

From a talent perspective, failing to upskill the marketing team to work alongside AI is a serious pitfall. Investing in training and fostering a culture of continuous learning is essential for the team to leverage AI tools effectively and stay ahead of the curve in the rapidly evolving marketing landscape.

Ignoring the insights gathered from case studies of AI applications in marketing—both successful and unsuccessful—is akin to walking through a minefield blindfolded. Learning from the experiences of others can help marketers avoid common errors and apply the best practices that others have painstakingly distilled from their trials and triumphs.

Lastly, a significant pitfall is the lack of a strategic vision for AI in marketing. AI should not be adopted just for the sake of being trendy. Marketers need a clear understanding of their objectives and how AI can help achieve them. This aligns the technology's application with the business's overall goals, ensuring that AI serves as a tool for success rather than a costly distraction.

By being cognizant of and actively avoiding these common pitfalls, marketers can better navigate the complexities of incorporating AI into their global strategies. The road ahead is brimming with potential, and those who approach AI with a thoughtful, informed, and careful strategy will be the ones to reap its most profound benefits.

Chapter 13:
The Road Ahead for AI in Global Marketing

As the horizon of global marketing broadens, the integration of artificial intelligence (AI) remains a shining beacon of progress, innovation, and limitless possibilities. This trajectory towards AI-enhanced marketing is not just an incremental step; it is a quantum leap that is reshaping the landscape with every passing moment. We stand at the cusp of a new era where data-driven insights, advanced analytics, and machine learning capabilities converge to offer a more personalized, efficient, and engaging marketing ecosystem.

Looking ahead, it is evident that AI will continue to magnify the efficiency of marketing strategies while challenging marketers to remain agile and informed. The field is ripe with opportunity, as AI enables us to understand consumer behavior and preferences with an unprecedented level of detail. This intimate knowledge empowers marketers to craft campaigns that resonate on a personal level, forging connections that transcend the traditional seller-consumer dynamic.

As we venture forward, the symbiosis between AI and content will only grow stronger. Algorithms adept at discerning consumer needs will guide content creation and curation, enabling a brand narrative that is both compelling and contextually relevant. The nuanced abilities of natural language processing will automate and refine the storytelling process, championing authenticity while harnessing the precision of machine learning.

Programmatic advertising, a realm already being revolutionized by AI, is poised for further transformation. Machines that learn and adapt to optimize ad bids and placements will offer a surgical precision in reaching audiences. These intelligent systems will track campaign performance with unparalleled accuracy, continually adjusting and improving to ensure maximum impact and return on investment.

Social media platforms, already teeming with AI applications, will witness deeper integration. Here, AI will act as both an ally and a compass, navigating the vast social landscape to amplify brand presence and engagement. By analyzing patterns and sentiments in real time, AI tools will refine influencer marketing strategies and maintain the pulse on brand reputation.

The customer experience is another domain where AI exhibits formidable potential. Personalized purchasing journeys, proactive customer service chatbots, and real-time recommendations are just the beginning. As AI grows more sophisticated, these experiences will become even more seamless, delighting customers with an understanding and responsiveness that feels nothing short of magic.

With the search arena, voice search optimization, and AI-influenced algorithms will redefine how we connect with information. The capability to predict and shape search intent will create a harmonious relationship between content creators and consumers, with AI as the conduit that aligns interests and intent with precision.

In e-commerce, AI's impact is transformative. Through sophisticated algorithms, online shopping will become an even more tailored and immersive experience. AI's insights into inventory, supply chain, and consumer trends will construct a landscape where the right product meets the right customer at the right time, with ease and efficiency.

However, amid this enthusiasm, we must navigate the delicate balance between personalization and privacy. As marketers, it is our duty to harness the power of AI ethically, fostering trust and ensuring that consumer data is protected and used respectfully. This will require vigilance and a proactive stance on regulatory compliance as norms evolve in tandem with technological advancements.

The global market is a tapestry of diverse cultures and consumer behaviors. AI, with its dynamic learning abilities, provides the toolset to adapt and localize marketing strategies on an unprecedented scale. By integrating cultural sensitivities and local trends into AI models, brands can establish a resonant voice across different regions without losing their core identity.

Success in this AI-augmented marketing landscape is not just about the tools we use but also about the people who wield them. Marketers must continually update their skill sets, embracing an ever-evolving mix of analytical prowess and creative thinking. AI competency needs to be fostered within teams, making ongoing learning and adaptability cornerstones of professional development.

The case studies of AI in marketing that pepper our history are both instructional and cautionary tales. They inform us of the innovative potential of AI when applied effectively while underscoring the pitfalls of misjudgement and over-reliance. Learning from these lessons is invaluable as we write the next chapter in the annals of marketing's evolution.

To stay ahead, we must be pioneers, trailblazers who boldly experiment with AI while grounded in strategic thinking. This path forwards is not without its risks, but the rewards — a deeper understanding of our customers, more resonant campaigns, and the unparalleled efficiencies AI affords — are worth the endeavor.

In closing, the road ahead for AI in global marketing is bright with promise. It beckons us to innovate, to think critically about not just the potential but also the implications of artificial intelligence. As marketers, we are at the vanguard of this exciting journey, responsible for shaping a future where AI not only enhances our abilities but also enriches the human experience. It is a journey that we undertake not just with sophisticated algorithms and datasets, but with the creativity, insight, and ethical foresight that define us as professionals.

Indeed, as the wheels of AI-driven marketing continue to turn, propelling us into unchartered territories, our mandate is clear: adapt, innovate, learn, and lead. This is the road ahead — an exhilarating expedition where the juncture of human ingenuity and artificial intelligence will redefine what we thought possible, and in doing so, unquestionably redefine global marketing itself.

Chapter 14:
AI Marketing Technology Glossary

Continuing our exploration into the transformative world of AI in global marketing, it's essential to foster a deeper understanding of the vernacular that forms the backbone of this domain. The glossary at hand serves as a navigational tool, bringing clarity and insight to the complex terms and concepts you will encounter as you delve into the intricate relationship between AI and marketing.

A.1 Terms and Definitions

Grasping the lexicon of AI-driven marketing is the first step toward innovation and thought leadership. Here, we will illuminate the terminology that you, the marketer, entrepreneur, or student, will need to navigate the revolutionized landscape of global marketing strategies.

Algorithm: *A set of rules or procedures for solving problems, often used by AI to process data and make decisions.*

Artificial Intelligence (AI): *The branch of computer science that aims to create systems capable of performing tasks that normally require human intelligence, such as visual perception, speech recognition, decision-making, and language translation.*

Chatbot: *An AI program that simulates conversations with human users, especially over the internet, to provide customer service or information.*

Data Mining: *The practice of examining large databases in order to generate new information and identify patterns.*

Deep Learning: *A subset of machine learning involving neural networks with many layers, allowing computers to identify complex patterns in data.*

Machine Learning: *A type of AI that provides systems the ability to automatically learn and improve from experience without being explicitly programmed.*

Natural Language Processing (NLP): *The field of AI that focuses on the interaction between computers and human language, particularly how to program computers to process and analyze large amounts of natural language data.*

Neural Network: *A network or circuit of neurons, or in a modern sense, an artificial neural network composed of artificial neurons or nodes.*

Personalization: *The process of tailoring a service or a product to accommodate specific individuals, sometimes tied to groups or segments of individuals.*

Predictive Analytics: *The use of data, statistical algorithms, and machine learning techniques to identify the likelihood of future outcomes based on historical data.*

Programmatic Advertising: *An automated method of buying and selling ad inventory through an exchange, connecting advertisers to publishers.*

Sentiment Analysis: *Also known as opinion mining, it refers to the use of natural language processing, text analysis, and computational linguistics to identify and extract subjective information from source materials.*

SEO (Search Engine Optimization): *The practice of increasing the quantity and quality of traffic to your website through organic search engine results.*

A.2 Further Reading and Resources

Expanding your knowledge beyond these definitions and into the complex interplay of strategies and technologies is paramount. The further reading and resources provided will equip you with a comprehensive understanding, empowering you to leverage AI for your marketing initiatives effectively.

"AI Marketing Essentials" - A compendium for marketers seeking a foundational understanding of AI applications in the field.

"The Data-Driven Marketer's Guide" - A resource focusing on the importance of data analytics, consumer insights, and how AI enhances decision-making.

"Strategies for AI-Powered Personalization" - An insightful exploration of how AI can tailor experiences to individual customer preferences and behaviors.

"The Future of Customer Engagement" - Predictive trends and insights into how AI is shaping customer-brand interactions in real-time.

"AI and Programmatic Advertising" - Understanding the automated, algorithm-driven future of ad buying and placement.

"Regulatory Compliance in AI" - A guide to navigating the legal landscape of AI in marketing, with a focus on privacy and ethical concerns.

With these resources and the defined glossary terms, your journey through the AI marketing realm will be informed and forward-thinking. Innovation awaits at the intersection of AI technology and strategic marketing, where your newfound knowledge will enhance global competitiveness and drive success in the ever-evolving marketplace.

A.1 Terms and Definitions As we delve deeper into the intricacies of AI in global marketing, it's imperative to establish a foundation of shared understanding. A precise grasp of terms and definitions paves the way for a clear and insightful discourse. This section serves as your lexicon, a repository of essential terminology that will frequently surface throughout our exploration.

Let's begin with **AI (Artificial Intelligence)**, a term that sits at the base of our exploration. AI is the simulation of human intelligence processes by machines, especially computer systems. These processes include learning, reasoning, and self-correction, which are essential for AI to effectively evolve and refine marketing strategies.

Within the realm of AI, we encounter **machine learning (ML)**. ML is a subset of AI that equips computers with the ability to learn and improve from experience without being explicitly programmed. In marketing, this translates to algorithms that can predict consumer behavior and personalize content, among other capabilities.

The concept of **natural language processing (NLP)** is also significant. This technology enables the interaction between computers and humans using natural language. It's the backbone of AI-driven content creation, allowing for the generation of human-like text, voice recognition, and sentiment analysis.

Moving on, the term **predictive analytics** is central to our discussions. It refers to the use of data, statistical algorithms, and machine learning techniques to identify the likelihood of future outcomes. Marketers utilize this to forecast consumer behavior and tailor their strategies accordingly.

A frequently mentioned instrument in this AI symphony is the **chatbot**. A chatbot is a computer program designed to simulate conversation with human users, especially over the internet. They enhance customer service and engagement by providing quick, AI-powered responses to queries.

Another core term is **programmatic advertising**. It's the use of AI to automate the buying and placement of ads, enabling more efficient targeting and real-time bidding. This innovation in advertising ensures marketers are reaching the right audience at the optimum time and price.

Personalization engine is the next term in our glossary. It refers to AI platforms that analyze dozens of data points to deliver individualized content, product recommendations, or experiences to users, augmenting customer satisfaction and brand loyalty.

With data being the lifeblood of AI, the concept of **data mining** is crucial. It involves the process of discovering patterns and extracting information from large datasets. For marketers, this means uncovering new opportunities and understanding customer segments more intimately.

The discussion on data brings us to **big data**, describing extremely large data sets that may be analyzed computationally to reveal patterns, trends, and associations. In marketing, big data is the canvas on which AI paints a picture of the global consumer landscape.

When it comes to content, the phrase **content curation** is of essence. It's the process of gathering, organizing, and presenting digital content on specific subjects. AI aids in this by filtering and personalizing content for users based on their preferences and behaviors.

Sentiment analysis, another term on our list, is the process of computationally identifying and categorizing opinions expressed in a piece of text. This allows marketers to gauge public opinion and emotional responses related to products or brands on social media and other platforms.

An indispensable tool in the kit is the **virtual assistant**, sometimes referred to as an intelligent personal assistant. It's an application that understands natural language voice commands and completes tasks for the user. Marketers leverage this AI capability to enhance online shopping experiences and customer service.

The term **SEO (Search Engine Optimization)** also warrants attention. With AI's increasing influence, SEO now goes beyond keyword stuffing to understanding the nuances of search engine algorithms, delivering content optimization strategies that resonate with AI-driven search engines.

Last but not least, we encounter **cross-cultural adaptation**. This is the process by which a product, service, or content piece is adapted to accommodate different cultural norms and preferences. In AI-driven marketing, this ensures that strategies are respectful of, and tailored to, diverse global audiences.

These are but a few of the terms that will be our constant companions as we navigate the dynamic intersection of AI and global marketing. A solid understanding of these definitions will provide clarity and context, enriching our journey through the subsequent chapters.

A.2 Further Reading and Resources In the pursuit of deepening one's understanding and competence in the integration of artificial intelligence into global marketing strategies, it is vital to arm oneself with extensive knowledge and resources. This section has been meticulously curated to provide you with a comprehensive list of books, articles, research papers, and digital resources that can serve as a beacon of insight in this ever-evolving domain.

For those who seek a more profound comprehension of AI's foundation and capabilities, seminal books on artificial intelligence principles are indispensable. Primary texts often feature interdisciplinary perspectives blending computer science, cognitive psychology, and data analytics. These resources not only shed light on the mechanisms of AI but also provide contextual applications which can be adapted to marketing.

Equally crucial is the understanding of consumer behavior analysis through the lens of predictive analytics. Explore academic journals and case studies focusing on personalization and consumer insights via AI. Look for scholarly articles that dissect the balance between data-driven marketing strategies and ethical considerations, as these will prepare one to navigate the complex landscape of consumer privacy and data protection.

How AI is revolutionizing content creation should be another key area of focus. Investigate online resources, case studies, and whitepapers that illustrate natural language processing advancements and their impact on content marketing. Also, creative processes augmented by machine learning can be studied through interactive webinars and digital workshops, which often provide dynamic examples of AI in action.

Further delve into AI's role in programmatic advertising by reading up on the latest algorithmic advancements. Experts often publish their findings and perspectives in industry reports and blogs, which are ripe with actionable insights. These writings are invaluable for understanding how AI can optimize ad targeting, bidding strategies, and campaign measurements for heightened efficiency and effectiveness.

Social media strategies are constantly being reshaped by artificial intelligence, and there is no shortage of online courses and tutorials that showcase the use of AI tools for better engagement. Keep abreast of these developments by following leading industry influencers, many of whom share content regularly on how best to leverage AI for competitive advantage.

In customer experience and support, AI's influence is profound and fast-evolving. Read customer success stories and whitepapers provided by AI service providers to understand the practical application of chatbots and virtual assistants. Moreover, engage with interactive platforms that simulate AI-based customer journey mapping to visualize and anticipate customer needs.

Considering how AI is changing the SEO landscape, staying informed about voice search optimization and search algorithm updates is critical. SEO blogs, webinars, and online communities are rich in resources and discussions that dissect these topics and offer strategic approaches to adapting content for AI compatibility.

For a practical understanding of AI in e-commerce, attend virtual conferences or workshops where industry leaders present new tools and strategies. Exploring detailed case studies of AI in inventory management, personalized shopping, and visual commerce are avenues through which professionals can envisage the future of online shopping.

Privacy and trust in marketing take on new dimensions with AI. Policy papers, legal reviews, and academic articles specializing in AI and privacy can offer perspectives that help marketers strike a balance between personalization and privacy, ensuring compliance and fostering trust.

When considering global marketing, reading about cross-cultural adaptation of AI technologies is invaluable. Explore international case studies and global market reports that focus on localizing AI strategies while maintaining consistency. Learning about cultural differences in

AI application will enhance one's ability to scale marketing efforts across diverse geographical landscapes.

Building AI talent and marketing skills requires a mixture of theory and practice. Online certification courses, hands-on workshops, and leadership training seminars are all avenues to build AI competence within marketing teams. Additionally, autobiographies and interviews with leading marketing professionals can provide personal insights on leading in the AI-enhanced marketing era.

Inspiration can be found in assessing real-world applications of AI in marketing. Therefore, identifying a slew of case studies that review both successful and failed AI implementation can serve as a learning tool. Best practices can often be found written up in industry reports and strategy documents prepared by marketing think tanks and consultancies.

Lastly, staying updated with the latest trends and predictions for the future of AI in marketing is a process of continual learning. Future-focused marketing magazines, trend analysis, and forward-thinking blogs offer snippets of what lies ahead, and how one might strategically prepare.

In summation, your journey through mastering AI-driven marketing strategies is complemented and enriched by these further readings and resources. They represent not just the foundation for present knowledge but also a launchpad for future innovation, equipping you with the intellectual tools to both understand and shape the future of global marketing in the age of AI.

www.ingramcontent.com/pod-product-compliance
Lightning Source LLC
Chambersburg PA
CBHW051244050326
40689CB00007B/1064